WAY OF LIFE AND IDENTITY

Edited by Anthony Jackson

SOCIAL SCIENCE RESEARCH COUNCIL

The Social Science Research Council (SSRC) is a body set up by Royal Charter for the promotion of social science research. Its functions are:

to encourage and support by any means research in the social sciences by any other person or body

to make grants to students for postgraduate instruction in the social sciences

to carry out research in the social sciences

to provide and operate services for common use for carrying on such research

to provide advice and to disseminate knowledge concerning the social sciences.

1 Temple Avenue, London, EC4Y 0BD   Tel: 01-353-5252

NORTH SEA OIL PANEL

This paper is one of a series produced under the auspices of the North Sea Oil Panel. The Panel was set up by the SSRC in 1975 to promote research into the social, economic and political impact on Scotland of North Sea Oil developments. The Panel, now in its final year, has sponsored a wide range of enquiries in Universities and other institutions. The results of some of these studies are being published as books or journal articles. In many instances however an alternative form of publication is more appropriate, and it is to provide such a medium that this series of Occasional Papers has been launched.

F M Martin

The views expressed in this paper are those of the authors and not necessarily those of the Social Science Research Council or its North Sea Oil Panel.

COMPOSITION OF THE PANEL

CHAIRMAN   Professor F M Martin,
Department of Social Administration and
Social Work, University of Glasgow.

MEMBERS   Professor T Daintith,
Department of Public Law, University of Dundee.

Professor J Eldridge,
Department of Sociology, University of Glasgow.

Professor M Gaskin,
Department of Political Economy,
University of Aberdeen.

Professor Sir R Grieve.
formerly Professor of Town and Regional Planning,
University of Glasgow.

Dr A Jackson,
Department of Social Anthropology,
University of Edinburgh.

Sheriff A MacDonald,
Shetland.

ASSESSORS   Miss B D Baker
Scottish Development Department.

Mr C Baxter,
Scottish Economic Planning Department.

Mr R Storey,
Highlands and Islands Development Board.

SECRETARY   Dr F Miller,
2 The Square,
University of Glasgow, G12.
Tel: 041-339-6563.

F O R E W O R D

One of the research priorities established by the North Sea Oil Panel was to take a fundamental look at what is meant by 'way of life'. To this end the Panel adopted two approaches: (1) a desk-study of the literature combined with intensive fieldwork in three areas, (2) a series of seminars on Way of Life.

This publication stems from one of the five seminars that have been held regularly since early 1979 in Edinburgh, convened by Dr Anthony Jackson. The aim of the seminars was to bring together everyone who had been conducting social anthropological fieldwork in Scotland recently. In this way it was hoped that informed discussions could be held on how oil-developments have affected way of life in different parts of Scotland.

The seminar discussions have been wide-ranging and have covered many aspects of way of life, not all of which were directly connected with oil-related activities. The papers presented to the seminars were essentially 'work in progress' reports and should not be read as completed pieces of research. Nevertheless it was felt that the papers deserved a wider circulation because of their intrinsic interest to a larger audience.

WAY OF LIFE AND IDENTITY

CONTENTS

Reflections on Way of Life
by Anthony Jackson

There are numerous ways in which life can be described:
e.g. the crofter's life, the crofting way of life, the quality
of crofting life, the crofter's standard of living. Naturally
all these versions are saying something different and to
achieve an understanding of these various measures of crofting
life we need to employ different criteria. In a sense all
these are comparative accounts, in particular the last two where
the amenities available and their quantity are compared with
other categories of people. An account of the crofter's life
may perhaps best be done in factual terms of how a crofter
copes with earning his living and how he spends his time.
As regards the way of life the focus narrows to the pattern
of a crofter's life and seeks to understand the meaning that
his life has for him. This last description is the most
difficult and hence has caused more controversy than the
others.

The first thing to note is that we need an adjective to
single out whose way of life is to be described. We cannot
discuss way of life in the abstract since the assumed patterns
of behaviour have to belong to somebody. The second point is,
then, how do we discover which adjective it is meaningful to
use? Of course, we may wish to know about the crofting way
of life but is this as easy as it sounds? The following
discussion takes up a number of points to see what is involved in making the attempt to describe way of life. We
will/

will begin by making a tentative definition and see where
that leads us.

A preliminary definition:

The concept 'way of life' denotes a bundle of routines,
values and feelings associated with a particular category of
persons, who are defined according to occupation, territory
and/or time, <u>as opposed to a similar but different category of
persons</u>, defined likewise, either implicitly or explicitly.

Before considering the elements of the above definition
it is worth dwelling upon the crucial importance of the
relativity embedded in the definition. It follows that there
can be no such thing as a <u>general</u> way of life and that all
usages of the concept make the implicit assumption that the
way of life under discussion is opposed to another way of
life which is inferior or superior, as the case might be.
Thus the concept is basically a value judgement and hence is
not objective, which means that no scientific definition can
be discovered. This fact partially accounts for the lack of
agreement on what the concept <u>really</u> means. In other words,
'way of life' is a comparative statement, like all other
value judgements. Aside from the actual scale of values involved in making such a judgement, it is important to ask
when and why these statements are called for. An obvious
answer to this is that way of life assertions are made when
the values in question are felt to be threatened - by other
values, of course. The occasions for this clearly arise in
times of <u>rapid</u> social change that characterize our present
century. Hence we should not be surprised that the concept
is frequently used nowadays by persons who feel themselves
beleaguered by alien values.

There/

There is a corollary to be drawn here. Just as
categories of persons (i.e. those who find themselves in
the same boat) feel threatened so do individuals, and
this is expressed in the so-called problem of identity-
crisis. Thus 'way of life' assertions and doubts about
self-identity are closely related. Here, these issues
will be treated separately to begin with, but it is as
well to point out that they are both symptoms of some
deeper malaise in the human psyche, and that they have a
common root. Put very simplistically, people have to
relate their lives in a meaningful way to others and this
involves obtaining confirmation that what they are doing
is 'correct', 'purposeful', etc. Such a justification
is made with reference to a scale of values and hence one
seeks out those who hold similar views. In so-called
traditional societies, it is assumed that everyone acts
according to a similar set of values and therefore few
doubts arise about the legitimacy of what one does or who
one is. Although this assumption may not be completely
true it nevertheless makes the point that one did not have
to seek far for support. In today's plurality of values
this moral bolstering-up of one's activities in a meaningful way is much harder to find and it accounts for the
current search for support that simply was not so necessary
in former times. This results in what one could characterize
as the search for group support (way of life) and self-
support (identity). Problems, however, arise since category
and group are not necessarily the same while the modern cult
of individuality necessarily opposes any identification with
anybody else. It is these dilemmas facing people that lie at
the/

the basis of our present discussion and because few satisfactory resolutions exist the resulting debates often take a
polemical and rhetorical form in order to prove oneself to be
in the right. In these circumstances it is not really surprising that 'way of life' and 'identity' have to be deliberately vague and ill-defined if they are to be effective
weapons of persuasion for, otherwise, their emotive force
would be largely lost if they were given too precise a
definition. As will be discussed later, the concept of
community also falls into this category of emotive words
and also defies an objective definition. These remarks are
by no means to be interpreted as belittling the importance
of these concepts in daily life. Their very vagueness is
their chief strength and they do express a real concern.

The concept 'way of life' is a portmanteau word to
denote a bundle of routines, values and feelings associated
with a particular category of people. As such, the concept
may be used equally by a member of the people concerned or
by an outsider. From the inside, the boundaries are set by
all those who act and feel the same which can lead to
sharply-delimiting the areas that are considered to be
similar to one's own and hence this gives rise to an
apparently great multitude of 'ways of life'. From the
outside, such minutiae are likely to be overlooked in favour
of broadly characterizing 'way of life' mainly in terms of
routines and values that are widely held among certain social
categories.

The structural relativity of the way of life concept
can be seen with respect to three important parameters:
occupation, territory and time. Along each of these
dimensions for any specified 'way of life' one will find
an/

an implicit contrast class which highlights the parti-
cularities of meaning given by the attributive adjective
used e.g. rural as opposed to urban way of life. It
follows that some accounts of 'way of life' are more easily
described in negative terms, derived from the contrast class
e.g. "there is little crime here" - implying that there is
a lot of crime in the other way of life. However, because
there are many possible implicit contrast classes and as
these are not always articulated, the description of a
particular way of life may then appear ambiguous when
couched in such negative terms since they may have multiple
and conflicting reference classes, a point that will be
taken up when discussing territory.

A common feature to both the internal and external view
of way of life is the emphasis on work routines as its chief
characteristic because this seems both obvious and objective
e.g. 'the crofting way of life', 'the countryman's way of
life', 'the fisherman's way of life'. The disadvantage with
this type of attribution is that it may get confused with the
two other parameters of space and time. We often associate
occupations with territory and see in that description aspects
that are not necessarily there, for example, fishermen can
live in the town or country, as can miners, but our stereotypes may associate both fishermen and miners with small
villages only. Our conclusions about that way of life
though may still be justified even when we examine the life
or urban miners and fishermen. Likewise, the time dimension
is often confused in those instances when the adjective
'traditional' is attributed to such ways of life. Tradition
is not the essence of 'way of life' - only set routines are
essential. Whether such routines stretch back unchanged
into/

into the past is an <u>evaluation</u>, not an intrinsic part of way of life. To say that 'way of life' must be wholly traditional is to deny that any innovations or changes are possible, which is patently not the case anywhere today and probably never was the case. Certainly, some aspects, in such particular things as attitudes and values, may have been unchanged for long periods but this is another matter.

'Way of life' is always structurally relative to the point of contrast being made. Thus village A is different from village B but A and B are similar with regard to village C which is different and so on, right up to contrasts of national differences.

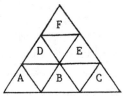 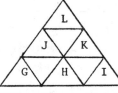 County

District

Village

Hence counties F and L differ from each other by the particular composition of the total ways of life contained in their respective villages A, B, C and G, H, I. The higher the level the more general are the supposed characteristics, which <u>pari passu</u> are then less-descriptive of the differences between A, B, and C at the lowest level. Thus while, e.g. Lanark and Ross could be broadly characterized as industrial versus rural counties such a generalization is only statistically true in aggregate and is not the case for all the villages and towns throughout the particular county. At the same time, because of the greater diversity contained at higher levels, it is probably incorrect to attach territorial adjectives to 'way of life' except as gross abstractions. Perhaps/

Perhaps a Lanarkshire way of life _is_ quite meaningless,
even by contrast, unless there is an emotive feeling that
territorial boundaries themselves are meaningful. So while
we may (but not necessarily clearly) contrast the British
and French way of life because of national feelings of
difference, there may be lesser areas where such feelings
of local patriotism are absent. It might be instructive to
consider what levels of abstraction are used:

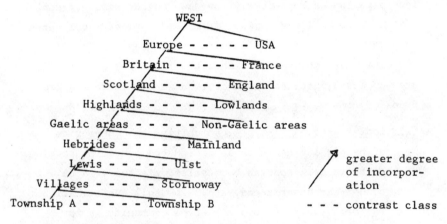

At each level there is a corresponding contrast class
and comparisons are normally kept to the same level so that
one does not compare Lewis with the Lowlands in general but
with, say, the Lothians. This discrimination, if made, also
involves a historical dimension besides a factual account of
set routines since an explanation of the differences is required and this is commonly made in purely historical terms.
History can be used as a legitimising myth for current social
practices at any level whether or not there is any causal
connection with the past. This justificatory element in one's
'way of life' need not be taken at its face-value since it is
an evaluation and not an explanation that is being offered.
This/

This means that all the details of the past cannot possibly
be seriously considered for every 'way of life' investigated
and so this rules out-of-court such macro-distinctions as
Scottish v English way of life. The problem now becomes:
which level of analysis do we wish to examine? Putting it the
other way round we can ask which category of people are involved
in 'our' or 'their' 'way of life'? These will be incorporative
categories in any case but it is suggested that the level of
investigation be kept fairly low down on the scale of contrasts.

Another ambiguity arises from the usage of local territory to describe way of life since that hinges on a prior
definition of 'community'. Thus the 'Shetland way of life'
presupposes a Shetland community. However, there are two
types of community:

(1) <u>Administration (A-type) communities</u> are <u>categories</u>
of people living in areas designated by administrative
criteria, e.g. parish boundaries, electoral wards,
school-catchment areas, etc. The sole qualification
for membership of such an A-type community is to
<u>reside</u> within the designated boundary.

(2) <u>Social (S-type) communities</u> are <u>groups</u> of people
designated by various criteria, e.g. religious
affiliation; party membership; linguistic, ethnic
or kinship ties, etc. The sole qualification for
membership of an S-type community is to <u>belong</u> to such
a group.

Any A-type community will contain one or more S-types.
Furthermore, A-type communities overlap since they are simply
categories and they will, because they are of bureaucratic
origin, show great similarities from place to place. In
addition/

addition, these A-type communities nest within a hierarchy
of ever-more inclusive categories, e.g. Morningside, Edinburgh,
Lothian, Scotland, UK, Europe, etc., as previously described.
This type of community is artificial, its needs are both prescribed and met from without. It is an imposed category whose
functions are single-stranded and hence it is treated mechan-
istically - as if all such communities were the same. The
problem is that such A-type communities are falsely assumed
to be integrated social communities or, even worse, that they
should be so.   This fallacy arises because there are certain
A-type communities (particularly in small rural areas) that
are unifocal, i.e. the several administrative boundaries
(religious, political, educational) coincide. In these
instances it is also possible to find there are only a few
S-type communities as well, i.e. people belong to the same
groups. This classical case is then held to be a 'true'
community with common interests and a common way of life,
since A and S-type communities merge. The error is to assume
that the characteristics of S-type communities are always
applicable to A-type communities. It is on this rock that
many notions of 'community' come to grief.

The point has to be laboured because this typical confusion of 'communities' is widespread and people hopelessly
try to reconcile them. 'Community' is a weasel-word which
should be avoided if possible but any replacement will also
fall into the same trap unless we are very careful.

The time-dimension has already been briefly mentioned
in connection with tradition but, as remarked earlier, this
is not an essential component of way of life. More problematical is the task of discovering when any particular way of
life/

life is, or was, followed. There is always an implicit
contrast - now : then - where the 'then' can either be in
the past or the future. Yet because 'way of life' implies
continuity, it must have had a past even though it may be
very shallow. When tradition is involved it may be evaluated
positively or negatively, as desirable or undesirable. Thus
it is important to discover how the use of 'way of life' links
the present with the past and the future but also when that
particular past was. As indicated previously, way of life is
invoked when the future seems threatening, it is rarely used
in stable situations because current practices are not
questioned and hence need no defence. So again, this
dimension is also relative and used contrastively.

The crystallisation of way of life ideas in people's
minds comes about by planting the seed of doubt that their
ways are not sacrosanct. Up to this point there is little
occasion to reflect on a defence of one's accustomed ways.
Indeed, way of life is not simply a set of routines, values
and attitudes that can be viewed separately but rather it
consists of an intimate and related set of ideas and
practices that are so closely interwoven that the very
practices evoke feelings and vice-versa. Thus it is
possible to call to mind one's own way of life by conjuring
up any number of ideas that can act as symbols for it - the
land, sea, church, the plough, Spring, harvest, the boat,
etc. Each idea or symbol can evoke the whole pattern of life
simply because it can be placed in a <u>known</u> routine, an ordered
whole. In so-called traditional societies, the daily rounds
are set, the human actions known, the progress of the year
is familiar and life may be seen and felt as predictable,
safe and secure. What are here called 'symbols' are so <u>only</u>
in/

in retrospect (and perhaps way of life, too can only be
thought of in contrast to the present) for in reality such
'symbols' are not perceived in that light when they are
part and parcel of living, which is a total whole.

Yet when called upon to describe one's way of life,
people may choose certain symbols in an apparently random
way which, however make perfect sense to their own group
since they can be fitted into the common background of
shared experience but which, to outsiders, remain only dis-
connected images. The point here is that way of life is
mediated by symbols that remain latent until called into
question and the responses thus invoked depend on <u>lived</u>
experience.

Such way of life symbols function in precisely the
same way as words do in poetry - they are evocative. It
may be no coincidence that there is at present a great
deal of poetry written in <u>dialect</u> which commemorates and
laments the passing of the old ways. In this connection
even language itself becomes a symbol for the way of life
that is threatened and hence poems in dialect have a doubled
power in defending one's ways. However, this poetic blossom-
ing is itself a sign that defeat is perhaps inevitable.

We have discussed three parameters of way of life -
occupation, territory and time - and touched on the question
of language but there are other dimensions such as culture
and class and ethnicity that could also be used as boundary
markers. In this discussion we are assuming there to be a
common cultural heritage and a single ethnic population,
to omit compounding the variables.

Now criteria generate categories, like class, which are
not groups of people in face-to-face interaction but are
simply/

simply the shared charateristics of people. Thus
occupational ways of life do not necessarily denote the
interaction of a group of people living together. In
real life people do live in groups but these may not be
occupationally 'pure' and hence a mixture of different
ways of life may co-exist in any given settlement. It is
important then to distinguish the type of interaction that
occurs between the followers of different ways of life.
Such interactions can vary along a continuum from complete
homogeneity to extreme heterogeneity and it also follows
that there is likely to be an increasing number of people
involved as we pass along this continuum, from small town-
ships to cities. Paradoxically enough, one finds that the
term 'community' is applied equally to both small and large
aggregates of people as if there was some common denominator
here, despite the evidence to the contrary. Ideally, one
would like to restrict 'community' to those people living
together and following a particular way of life but this
will not do in the face of what actually happens.

A distinction can be drawn such that community denotes
only those people with a common interest whether or not they
live together. Clearly some of those with a common interest
will also form groups if they do not live too far apart. One
could go further and define a community as those who share
overlapping interests and who also live near enough to each
other to interact on a face-to-face basis. In this definition
of community there are obvious parallels with way of life but
with the difference that the two concepts lie at polar extremes
from each other. Community lies at the voluntary pole of
behaviour while way of life is at the involuntary pole. This
could/

could be illustrated by saying that one can <u>join</u> a
community but one is <u>born and brought up</u> in a way of life.
From this it follows that 'community' is <u>not</u> necessarily
localized but a 'way of life' is. Hence a 'village community'
implies locally-bound interests common to all villagers <u>qua</u>
villagers, not that they have a <u>common</u> way of life. Incomers
may join a village community and defend it but they do not
have to share whatever ways of life that might be found there.
The thrust of this argument is that 'community' is not a
satisfactory criterion and that 'way of life' tends to be a
product of upbringing rather than a conscious decision to
adopt particular habits. Hence the criterion of 'a common
upbringing' is an important element in our discussion of
way of life.

If this criterion of upbringing or socialization is a
sound one, then it leads on to the question of schooling and
its influence on attitudes. Take, for example, the case of
small schools (which tend to be rural) and the position of
secondary schooling which may involve boarding in remote
areas. Although today education is the prime route out of
one's home milieu into a better qualified job, which almost
by definition would involve a different way of life, this
may not always have been the case. Before the raising of the
school-leaving age and the implementation of the 1944 Education
Act it could be that schooling unintentionally fostered the
ongoing way of life by simply bringing children together, yet
offering them no new opportunities. This is only a hypothesis,
but, if say, schooling had no great impact until 1950 then
only the under-40s are likely to have been affected. The
corollary being that <u>the</u> 'way of life' syndrome is only
meaningful to the over-40s, in the main. Another dimension
to/

to this is the mass-media which also affects attitudes.
One could postulate that films did not jar one's ideas
about one's 'way of life' because films were plainly dramatic and fictional - not to be taken seriously. However, TV
adds a realistic dimension which more convincingly displays,
often deliberately, other ways of life. This, together with
schooling, from the 1950's onwards, might have powerfully
affected the attitudes and values people held towards their
own 'way of life'. What is being suggested is that 'way of
life' only became problematical as a general phenomenon in
the last quarter century.

There is another set of factors that affect attitudes
towards 'way of life' and they are mobility and migration.
Mobility is the result of better communication, better jobs
and higher rates of employment while migration may be due to
fewer jobs and unemployment. To greatly oversimplify :
mobility is voluntary, migration is involuntary. The point
is that migration does not necessarily destroy one's
attitudes towards one's former way of life and hence these
memories may remain in exile-groups and even prompt return
to one's home, when one can. By contrast, mobility (often
school-engendered) need carry no such commitments and no
regrets. Although this suggestion may not be sound it prompts
the reflection that employment possibilities, at any given
time, may be crucial to people's view of their way of life
and that this depends very much on the life-careers of the
informants. In other words, in areas of high unemployment
there may be discrepant information on 'way of life' depending
on whether people have had continuous or intermittent residence
in a particular area, and also on how old they are. Thus per-
ceptions of 'way of life' as seen by returned migrants might
contain/

contain a romanticised view of the 'good old days' whereas those who remained might dismiss this 'traditional' view as not constituting their own view of the matter as it stands now. There may well exist a cognitive discrepancy among certain people, especially returned-migrants, who bemoan the changes <u>they</u> see to have happened, yet act as if the proper 'way of life' should be conducted according to the old lines they were once familiar with, failing to realize that the present way is the only path open to the inhabitants. I suggest that this could be another source of the current debate in 'way of life' which is often posed in terms of 'traditional' versus 'modern'. Briefly, this is a case of separating memories from experience, romance from reality - a hard problem for exiles and local patriots alike. We should not fall in the trap of confusing them ourselves. The moral here being that <u>continuity of experience</u> is an important element in 'way of life' if it is to be an accurate reflection of reality.

<u>Summary</u>:

The structural relativity of 'way of life' demands that we know:

(1) which social groups are involved i.e. we require to know the criteria by which they are delimited, their size, scope, interaction, etc.

(2) which features are stressed in

> (a) work patterns
>
> (b) values
>
> (c) feelings and experience.

The important elements of 'way of life' are the group, its purpose, its identity and its continuity - these must be elicited by informants who are 'placed' with regard to the groups/

groups discussed above, according to their age and experience
of the group.

Conclusions:

It may be found that even the way of life of one particular category e.g. crofting, will vary depending on local
circumstances and that no broad generalizations are possible.
Only when we have sufficient accounts will we be able to
judge this. It would be rash to assume that a single investigation could reveal all the basic features of a given way of
life.

A final observation

The discussion has touched in several places on a polarity
between voluntary and involuntary behaviour which are summar-
ized below:

Involuntary actions	Voluntary actions
(due to external pressures and often found in traditionalistic societies.)	(due to internal-individualistic motivations and found in modern societies.)
Ways of life . . . . .Communities (of interest)	
Migration . . . . .Mobility (geographical and social)	

The above distinctions are remarked upon because they
bring out some important contrasts. Thus, migration is closely
related to way of life as an intrinsic, albeit a reluctant, part
of traditionalistic society and is not a recent or separate
phenomenon. Similarly, in modern society, mobility is a
sine qua non of adapting to community life since each is a
product of individual striving for achievement. The difference
between these two poles is simply one of attitude and this
value-shift is an important aspect of our study that must be
borne/

borne in mind. It is here that a historical awareness must
be brought into the discussion.

Way of life is perhaps a cultural or aesthetic concept
which is not intrinsically capable of being tested by scientific measurement. The fact that cultural concepts refer to,
but do not encapsulate, human experience accounts for the
difficulty in reaching agreement about what they 'mean'. Such
concepts are a common coin of discourse because they refer to
recognizable areas of human experience that everyone has and
for which it is necessary to have a term in order to be able
to talk about it. The experiences in question lie in the
realm of feeling and not in the realm of knowledge and hence
we cannot 'know' the unknowable - we can only express it.
Thus 'way of life' falls into the same category as 'Art'
and 'Religion'. A person can intuitively understand the
concept 'way of life' as applied to his life but might find
it hard to translate into words what this concept means to
him. So we may argue that the concept 'way of life' belongs
to an intuitive part of our vocabulary which renders it in-
susceptible to strict formulation. This is not a new problem
to the social sciences but it is difficult to resolve. We
may decide to choose a description of the objective conditions
that frame human action, according to the roles of the actors
concerned, but the result is often static and lifeless, even
unrecognizable to the actors themselves. Alternatively, we
may choose to describe the individual's life from within,
like a biography, but while such descriptions are recognizable
they are too individualistic to be generalizable.

If neither an objective or a subjective description is a
completely valid way to understand 'way of life' we may have
to consider yet other ways of conveying the sense of a way of
life so that we can evoke an understanding. Since we are
dealing/

dealing with intuitions we need to use such methods that will call forth responses of recognition and the obvious ones are the use of novels and poetry to convey such situations and to evoke feelings.

The above suggestion flies in the face of the claims of social science research but we should not simply assume that every social topic can be fully investigated by the tools we happen to have at the moment. This is not to say that anthropological research cannot convey something of the flavour of a way of life but it may not be enough.

My final thought is that we should <u>complement</u> our studies with a piece of work that can evoke an awareness of what it is like to live according to a particular way of life. Such complementation must be more than a series of case studies, although these are helpful, since the aim must be to evoke the feeling that this is what it means to <u>live</u> that way of life. Now whether this work should be a short story, a novel or a poem is debateable but it might be worth pursuing the idea. At present, our accounts lack that spark of life which awaken a recognition of reality. It may be no bad thing to extend our own awareness of the possibility that better ways of conveying our knowledge exist than our current standard practices.

Identity

by Anthony   Jackson

'. . . and whatsoever the man called every
living creature, that was the name thereof.'
(Genesis 2: 19)

1.   A universal feature of mankind is a desire to give names
to things and persons so that wherever man goes he bestows a
name on what he sees. Thus the less transitive features of
the world such as 'hills, standing lakes and groves' all
receive a name which often outlasts the givers; this is a
boon to students of place-names but it also suggests that
there is a continuing entity called 'Caithness'. Now naming
as opposed to classification serves the purpose of practical
orientation and can be quite arbitrary, as long as it does
not lead to confusion. Hence naming is a way of discriminating things but it also enables us to group things together
since we learn that certain names have similar features as
bluebell, daisy, tulip, rose, violet, etc. One mode of
grouping these particular names together is to associate
them with flowers, but they may also refer to girls, and even
to cows. Which set of names apply will depend on the context
but the point is that names may have multiple references.
There are, then, different styles in naming which are culturally
determined and we must recognize these; thus none of the above-
mentioned names are ever applied to rivers, men or birds. All
this is commonplace yet we often overlook the explicit and
implicit rules of naming when we discuss the properties of
those entities that we identify by name. The problem lies
in the covert transference of postulated essential features
from/

from one set of names to another e.g. from rose to Rose
where ideas of beauty, fragrance and delicacy are attributed
to a woman on the sole basis of the name. Although this
example may be laughable, nevertheless we often operate on
this basis.

This essentialist basis of naming whereby it is assumed that
names are not simply labels but are descriptive of some core
feature is at the heart of the problem of identity. In other
words, when we discuss identity we are concerned with something
that is the same (q.v. idem, the same) and the problem resides
in isolating the elements of that sameness. In addition we
tend to assume a continuity of these elements, so we also
look for permanence. It was of course Plato who put forward
the essentialist view of the nature of things which has long
continued to be used in the Western tradition. We are not so
much concerned here with things per se but with people, and
the difficulty is to isolate anything in the flux of human
experience that is identifiable. With the rejection of the
concept of 'soul' there is little internal evidence of any
essential component of man and this has forced a crisis of
identity upon us. As a result we tend to use 'objective'
features of identification in our search for our 'essential'
nature, or to put it another way, today we seek our identity
outside ourselves rather than look within. All the same,
the quest for identity is a moral quest inasmuch as we
impute moral qualities to that identity however defined.
At bottom identity is a moral quality and our search is
basically one of justification. As we shall see in the
following discussion, all the characteristics employed in
identification are moral judgements either implicitly or
explicitly.

This/

This introduction serves to highlight the importance
of naming, the essentialist bias to our processes of
identification, and the moral judgements that we bring to
bear upon that identity.

2.   'Only connect . . .' (E M Foster)

The concept 'identity' is ambiguous for, when applied
to people, it has two contradictory meanings : sameness and
difference, viz:

(a)   a person identifies himself with another person, group
      or idea.

(b)   a person is identified by that which distinguishes him
      from everyone else.

These two aspects to a person's identity may be termed:

(a)   self-reflexive - when it refers to the way a person
                       defines or expresses his own identity

(b)   denotative   - when it refers to the way a person's
                       identity is established by other people.

Both ways of identification comprise two sets of characteristics.

(1)   observable characteristics

            i.   Badges (clothes, insignia, language,
                  natural features, etc.)

            ii.   Actions (mode, type and style of
                  behaviour)

            iii. Declarations (statements, claims,
                  pledges, etc.)

(2)   inferred characteristics

            i.   Loyalties.

            ii.   Intentions.

            iii. Attitudes and ideology.

A/

A complicating factor is that either mode of identification (self-reflexive and denotative) also contains both
a conscious and an unconscious dimension. Thus an individual
may deliberately strive to express a particular kind of
identity yet simultaneously reveal, unawares, another identity.
Likewise an observer may impose an identity upon someone (e.g.
a stereotype) either intentionally or by 'instinct' - i.e.
unconsciously. The difficulty, then, lies not only in
assessing the sets of characteristics as being true or
false but in checking these against one's own impressions.
What we have in the identification process is similar to a
pair of distorted mirrors facing each other - each image of
an object between the mirrors is reflected again and again,
so that it does not take many reflections before the object
is quite unrecognizable. Our difficulty quite simply is the
reverse fact that the characteristics of identity we observe
are only the images and our problem is to reconstruct the
shape of the object which we cannot see - we are back in
Plato's cave; sitting by the fire, looking at the shadows
moving on the wall.

The point of the above metaphoric comparison is simply
to stress the fact that we cannot take characteristics of
identity at their face value. Each person is, in a way,
reflected by others around him and the process of identity
building is a dialectical one. It is not a question of noting
the facts and coming up with the answer since there are
possibly no clear-cut ways of arriving at the identity of
anyone, only approximations can be attempted. This elusive-
ness of identity-fixing is why it puzzles and perplexes people
because they assume it ought to be possible to find one's
identity fairly easily and only then they discover the
difficulties. The same thing can be said about 'way of life'
which may be why that is equally problematical.

3./

3.   'Know your enemy' (Clausewitz)

A common method of identification is stereotyping.
This is really a way of classifying people as being the
same on the basis of some allegedly key feature such as
ethnic group, sex, age, or occupation. The drawback to
stereotyping is that it is simplistic, being based on
fragmentary information, hearsay and partial observation.
The reason why it is employed is precisely because it is
easy and one can pigeon-hole large numbers of people without
effort. Because stereotyping is classifying it inevitably
draws sharp distinctions between classes of discriminating
features which are shown up to be too coarse when one
actually considers individuals closely. Thus we get the
absurdity of such statements as 'All people from Aberdeen
are miserly but all the Aberdonians I know are generous'.
This contrast between stereotypes and denotative identification may be clarified by noting that stereotyping is an
inclusive process of assimilating people to one standard
type whereas denotative identification discriminates and
gives a person a distinct place in a network of relationships. In other words identification is not to be confused
with classification and the stereotyping of persons into
distinct types but, rather, it should be thought of as
mapping a person on to a set of variables. The difference
is that denotative identification is <u>not</u> objectifying but
subjectifying - ideally. This does not mean, of course,
that people resist stereotypes when they make denotative
identifications - they often do not - but this is rarely
done when they consider their friends and close neighbours.
Stereotypes, real or assumed, apply to strangers only.

4.   'Know thyself' (Socrates)

It is self-identity and the identity of the people
that we interact with most which are of prime concern to us
here since we wish to discover the process whereby identity
is achieved and maintained in face-to-face interaction.

Identity should be distinguished from individuality,
which is more a question of personal style. Thus our roles
may be an indicator of our identity since they are socially
given and can be used to differentiate us if roles are
articulated according to some common framework. But as we
may all interpret these roles differently our individuality
lies here, even if we can never escape our given roles.
Generally, our role behaviour makes use of conventional rules
which enable other people to draw inferences about our likely
behaviour and hence form some opinion about our identity -
what are we _really_ like (shades of Plato again!)

To return to the beginning, our denotative identification
begins with our given name and even if we are not known by it
(e.g. if we have a nickname), at least we have all got one.
This name identifies us, for it not only distinguishes us from
all others having different names but it also links us to
those with the same name. In our society we receive patron-
ymics that link us to our fathers and their kinsfolk but we
are also given Christian names at a religious rite which may
happen to follow a set pattern e.g. the first son receives the
father's first name, the first daughter her mother's, the
second son the father's father's name, the second daughter
the mother's mother's name, etc. Naming after godparents
is also common. These usages are culturally determined and
they thereby associate children to certain individuals and
hence similarities are often sought in their behaviour
patterns as a result.

Underlying/

Underlying this connection between one individual
and another is an implicit psychological-genetic hypothesis
which posits inheritance of behavioural traits besides
physical characteristics. While this may be acceptable
today in terms of genetic theory it only applies to those
people who are genetically related. It should be pointed
out that this does not then explain the word-magic that also
associates godparents and godchildren or even other people
having the same name.

We also have another explanation of behaviour which is
made in terms of Nurture where similar circumstances are
held to account for similarities of behaviour. At a popular
level this hypothesis is manifested by associating character
traits to provenance e.g. 'Aberdonians are tight-fisted',
'Lewismen are lazy'. While there may be socio-historical
reasons for these judgements - essentially stereotypes -
there is a tendency to gloss over the circumstances and to
make a direct association between place and people, as if
the provenance of a person was a direct causal agent of
behaviour.

In short, identity judgements are based on name and
provenance and these two items of information act as signals
of identity. One's name connects one with a family and this
may be then connected with a place, whereby the reputation
of one is confirmed by the reputation of the other.

5.   The totemic illusion.

There are certain observable characteristics of identity
which may be called regional badges, which serve to locate people,
and these include clothes, insignia, dialect and appearance.
Clearly, dress is something we put on to announce who we are
and it is easy to list these, from official uniforms (like
postmen)/

postmen) to unofficial uniforms (like jeans and sweaters).
There are the obvious differences in clothing between the
sexes besides regional variations like kilts, turbans, and
yashmaks. The wearing of clothes may also reveal one's
identity unawares since much dressing is conventional and
the subtle differences that still exist may never strike
the wearer e.g. sophistication or lack of it in colour
combinations and even the use of perfumes and/or deodorants!

Besides clothes, there are various insignia like hair
style, rings, ornaments and badges (even tools of one's
trade) which may proclaim one's allegiance to some group or
category. One could extend the catalogue of visible signs
to include so-called status symbols like using particular
brands of car, or living in certain types of house, or
furnishing one's home in a defined way, or even adopting
certain styles of living. These symbolic statements are
quite important in defining one's identify.

Finally, we have the most obvious badge of identity -
dialect. We are all forced to use language and this at
once proclaims an important aspect of identity - one's
nationality and regional location (both spatially and in
the social-structural sense). Much play is made of language
in identifying others and we have developed quite subtle
(though often unconscious) methods of distinguishing people
according to the place we think they belong. This method is
closely linked to our stereotyping of people on the grounds
of their birthplace.

Without expounding further on these badges of identity
here it should be clear that many of these signs may be used
to deliberately deceive the onlooker. In other words we
often need to cross-check our various cues in order to
reassure ourselves that we have correctly perceived the
identity/

identity of the person. This process of double-checking
we also do when we listen to people's declarations and
statements of intent. In both cases we often use the
method of comparing the claims made implicitly by badges,
and explicitly by utterances, with what people in fact do
and how they behave. What we attempt to do is to construct
their identity on this basis. This is, in fact, what we do
for ourselves when we display observable or public signs of
identity.

It is worth drawing a parallel with ritual symbols.
Many such symbols are in fact material objects onto which we
project meanings. The virtue of such symbols in material
form is that they <u>persist unchanged over time</u> - they can out-
live their human makers and users. Similarly, we may
attempt to enshrine our identity in material form, and give
it substance, so to speak. Why, one may ask, do we erect
statues to important people or give their names to buildings
or streets? This concretization of identity may be our way
of making permanent that ineffable inner identity which
eludes all our attempts at definition.

6.   'He that findeth his soul shall lose it. . . ' (St. Matthew 10: 39)

Our quest for identity perhaps is a desire to anchor ourselves on some unmoving rock where we may feel secure against
the tides of change that sweep across our lives. Why else do
we turn to the past - to history - that which is fixed? Why
do we justify our behaviour against 'eternal' norms? Why do
we try to concretize ourselves with material things? One could
argue that modern man, in becoming individualised, automatically
suffers from anomie and hence searches for the 'lost' together-
ness of primitive man by creating special groups dedicated to
sets/

sets of ideals. Were this thought to be the case, the
remedy may be as false as the notion of the 'happy'
community of the Golden Age. Yet could it be that the
'problem' of identity is a modern one - something that
only co-exists with the pursuit of individualism? In other
words, does the cult of the individual create the problem
of identity? Well, obviously people have always had the
problem of 'them and us' but it may not have always caused
much difficulty. Our particular problem seems to be that
we are not too certain who we are any longer. The old
guidelines of kinship and territory are not so helpful in
this modern age, nor are newer notions of class and nation.
Underlying this whole discussion seems to be a human need
to belong - but to what?

Identity - sameness - is an expression of our need to
belong somewhere and to some group. Perhaps that is why we
are so fiercely loyal to that bit of earth where we were
born and bred and to the people that live there. This
identification with place is truly remarkable but, as we
have seen, it is something permanent - more or less.

Also the fact that one can imagine and symbolize makes
it possible for us to identify with causes, utopias and other
worlds where we may find a resting place and security in the
company of like-minded people.

Perhaps we need approval from our peers and recognition
for ourselves, which simply recognizes the fact of our dependence on others in sustaining our construction of our
identity. Just as society depends on collusion, so do we.
The limits of our identity are set by the group which recognizes us and the amount of tolerance allowed will obviously vary. Our attempts at identity management are signals
for/

for recognition as really belonging. Within a given language
frame, that is often geographically limited, we may be suffi-
ciently socialized not to suffer anomie and we can feel we
belong and hence feel secure within the group. Our deviations
from the norms are probably slight in comparison with those of
other groups with which we do not interact. That is to say,
our identity management is normatively governed and this is
what is of interest to us. Our souls or lives are not then
to be sought within, but without - in the group.

7.   'I am that I am'

This disquisition on identity seems perilously closer to
a sermon than to an anthropological discussion, and there are
probably good reasons that could be adduced for this. To a
certain extent the concept of identity is a metaphysical one
which philosophy and religion have long struggled with. In
more modern guise it is a concept that concerns our modern
metaphysicians - the psychologists.

As social anthropologists our interest in 'identity' is
probably confined to modern societies only as it seems to
have been unproblematic in the 'traditional' societies we
generally study. The connection with the equally modern
problem of 'way of life' is no coincidence since it is
generally symptomatic of societies undergoing change.
When tradition is questioned, so is identity - just as much
as way of life.

It has not been possible in this paper to follow through
all the efforts we make at constructing and maintaining an
identity. Reduced to its simplest it means aligning oneself
with 'us' as opposed to 'them'. This endeavour is essentially
a collective enterprise and there are certain rules which 'our'
side/

side uses to define ourselves. This differentiation is
mainly a latent one and it is by no means simple. We tend
to form groups in opposition to others depending on the
situation and therefore the criteria, and <u>hence</u> our identity
is also relative, whatever we may claim to the contrary.
In other words, our personal identity is not some quintessential
atom that remains constant - whatever we conceive our <u>self</u> to
be. Nevertheless we tend to assume that one (whatever that is)
is the same because our conscious awareness does not seem to
alter, despite the passing of the years.

What does happen to us is that we fall into routines of
behaviour that we and others associate with us. These
patterns are determined to a great extent by our fellows and
because these ways are routine, they are both easy and
'natural' to follow. If, then, we follow similar patterns
to our group we are likely to feel more secure, as they are
the accepted ways of behaving. It is only when we come
across alternative behaviour patterns that any doubts arise.
Hence cultural differences, when forced upon one's awareness,
may give rise to reinforced adherence to the norms of one's
own group. After all, threats to one's own meaning and
purpose in life are mainly posed by outsiders. Thus quite
often, unknown strangers are stereotyped - in generally
unfavourable terms. The function of such stereotypes is
mainly to dismiss or contain threats to one's own sense of
the intrinsic correctness of one's own behaviour and that of
one's group.

Identity-seeking behaviour is a defensive mechanism
against external threats. We identify others as potentially
helpful or otherwise, and the clues we seek are whether they
are in agreement with us on certain points of current or
future/

future action. Our display of identity signals is to
announce our intentions and also to seek their acceptance.
As indicated above, such signals may take many forms and
their display may often be encoded so that only similarly
minded or the well-informed can recognize them, e.g. slang,
nicknames, gestures, and even subtler cues of behaviour that
may be involved.

No ethnographic examples have been given here since my
main concern has been analytical. There is still more that
could be said on identity but this attempt must suffice to
indicate some of the reasons why it is an important problem
which faces us when we discuss 'way of life' and why we must
provide some tentative explanations for it.

N O T E:

The aim of the above two position papers (which were
circulated to participants before the seminar) was to
stimulate some reactions to the topics in question. They
were meant to serve as sounding-boards against which participants could make their own views heard. For this reason
many of my statements are couched in a provocative and
dogmatic fashion. It was not the intention that these
papers should be seen as "balanced" - they are meant to be
challenged.

Way of Life - Seeking an Identity
by Adrian Varwell

Five way of life themes have been identified in the
course of my research - the personal, corporate, cultural
historical and indicative themes, although I propose to
ignore the last theme at this stage since it represents
a specialised theme concerned with the quantification of
data relating to way of life and quality of life. In
examining the first four themes alone I am dealing with
four broad contexts in which social scientists, novelists
and pressure groups have used the phrase 'way of life'.
There is not the need to review here the wide range of
literature which supports these four themes: indeed, my
own discoveries continue, and the data from the three
local area studies which form part of my study in the
Highlands appear to support and inform this categorisation.
What is increasingly clear, however, is that each of
the four themes contain common elements: the same features
used to describe way of life appear in each of the four
themes. A few initial examples must suffice. The personal
theme projects way of life as a checklist used in an
introspective sense to identify self and one's position in
relation to one's social landscape. Thus, to one the Shetland way of life involves:

> "Doggedness, faith, patience, humour, honesty,
> trust, help freely given, an instinctive sense of
> what is right and just, a respect for human life
> and human dignity." (1)

To another, a social scientist:

> "One/

"One aspect of quality of life is 'What I am . . .
Superimposed . . . is what happens to me . . .
How do I feel about my life? How do I see others
and how do I compare myself and my lot with theirs?
How do I see the larger social system in which
these are embedded? And with what interpretations
and expectations do I see the past and the future?"(2)

To another, quality of life refers:

"Either to the conditions of the environment in which
people live or to some attribute of people themselves
. . . implying a comparison of what exists to some
more or less explicit standard of what ought to exist."(3)

This writer goes on to identify physiological needs, safety, a
sense of belonging and love, esteem, self-actualisation, knowledge and understanding, aesthetics and happiness as ingredients
in a good quality of life (4). In the context of ghetto culture
Hannerz defines life style as:

"The involvement of an individual with a particular
set of modes of action, social relationships, and
contexts." (5)

Richard Hoggart, defining working-class ways of life suggests
that individuals:

"are just 'not there', (they) are living elsewhere,
living intuitively, habitually, verbally, drawing
on myth, aphorism, and ritual". (6)

The common elements in each of these cases may be summarised
thus: a person's position relative to others in terms of
social relationships, status and life experiences; a person's
relationship to social institutions such as justice and social
norms; a relationship to the past and future; a resource
of myth, belief and ritual to inform the intuitions and habits
of the individual; all elements uniting to provide the individual with a sense of place, of belonging, of identity.

The corporate theme projects way of life as a symbol of
group life, as an articulation of concern about social change,
or/

or as a myth generated to create identity. Thus
Mackinnon sees Gaelic as:

> "providing a shared institution of group life
> through which an alternative way of life is
> developed. A shared and distinctive language
> may enable group morale and group identification
> to withstand the economic and social pressures
> which are destructive of viable social life . . ."(7)

In Wester Ross and Lewis the concern expressed about crofting,
Gaelic and religious observance in the face of oil development:

> "should be seen as an articulation about the
> wider issues of the erosion of the traditional
> way of life." (8)

In Shetland, Wills has suggested that the way of life of
the islands may be:

> "a myth, created to prove that Shetland is 'special'
> and deserves special protection from oil."(9)

To Naomi Mitchison the hallmarks of the Highland way of
life are:

> "Stability, courage, kindness and a sense of
> belonging together, of being able to call on
> one another in times of stress,"(10)

and she continues:

> "we value deeply a way of life that gives
> people a sense of identity and security of
> being part of a community." (11)

In Wales the way of life in a small village is described as:

> "an intricate network of community relations . . .
> with strong family links . . . a most neighbourly
> community with an unusually strong religious and
> cultural life. The . . . community is vigorous and
> lively and leads a satisfying and enviable existence
> beyond the reach of urbanization."(12)

Again the common elements may be seen in terms of relativities,
a group or community in relation to its neighbours, to
different stages of economic development, urbanisation or
cultural/

cultural decline, and as a means of fostering a separate
identity, a security, and a unique context of social interactions.

The cultural theme projects way of life as something
specially related to language or nationhood, and the emphasis
placed upon the special features of the Cymraeg or the
Gaeltachd for instance, gives another context in which way
of life is articulated. The Welsh way of life is defined
as:

> "a pattern of rural life in Welsh language
> communities . . . "(13)

and as a:

> "People . . . united . . . by a belief in their
> national identity and their common wish for
> survival through the culture, language and
> values . . . "(14)

In the Highlands the Gaelic way of life is seen as something
which is:

> "ecologically sound, capable of withstanding social
> or moral collapse . . . cherishing the land and
> its resources, promoting a satisfying culture for
> its people and again providing the world with a
> further example of successful response to
> adversity." (15)

In Barra:

> "the Gaelic language and its associated lore and
> culture seemed to have an important function in
> providing the symbols for the self-identification
> of this society as a community . . . Gaelic was
> strongly maintained as one of the means whereby
> a small community was enabled to be aware of itself
> as a distinguishable whole both in cultural and
> social terms." (16)

The common elements within the ethnic theme include all the
relativities identified within the corporate theme, but
further embrace language (above all else), national or
regional identity, and uniqueness in contra-distinction to
the/

the perceived uniform culture everywhere else.

The historical theme is found in the writings of northern Scottish writers (amongst others) and all emphasise the interdependence of past and present, and of the essential roles of landscapes, seasons, work routines, institutions and the human imagination, in fashioning the way of life of the peoples they write about (17). Novelists, however, are not alone. Emrys Jones, a social geographer, has written:

> "Militating against change is a universal feeling
> of reluctance to upset an existing way of life.
> To accommodate change some part of the existing
> pattern must go, and yet the entire structure
> must not be damaged." (18)

Therefore, he says:

> "Insofar as the past is enshrined in the present,
> much of this will be handed on to the future: not
> the trivial and the banal . . . but the fundamental
> and deep-rooted values that are basic to it."(19)

In the same vein a Government working party states:

> "We want to provide for the future, live in the
> present, and keep some reminders of the past.
> We want roots, we want security, we want to
> belong."(20)

Naomi Mitchison states that an important element in the Highland way of life is the sense of continuity:

> "which is lost elsewhere,"

a sense maintained because:

> "history is personally real in the Highlands.
> People know who their ancestors were and how,
> through their ancestors they tie into the past
> and history, just as they must tie into the
> future through their decendants."(21)

Again there are common elements of relativity, in this context to time, to the environment, and to processes of change; and elements of identity, security and regional distinctiveness.

There/

There may now be seen to be four broad common elements
within each of the four way of life themes, relativity,
identity, security and exclusivity. Relativity denotes the
means by which way of life is used to define an individual,
a group, a cultural minority or a point in time in relation
to society, the nation, the predominant culture on the
passage of history, as a process of taking bearings on fixed
landmarks from a ship on a restless sea. Security suggests
a refuge of immovable sameness in the midst of change, that
by articulating concern about a way of life and by fighting
to preserve it, people grope for a safe haven. Such people
are experiencing a form of anomie:

> "characterized above all by a fundamental and tragic
> insecurity . . . the insecurity of the hopelessly
> disoriented. They have lost the ground on which they
> stood, the ground of their former values. Usually it
> happens when they have lost also their former environ-
> ment, their former connections, their social place,
> their economic support." (22)

Exclusivity is manifest in the expression of ways of life
which seek to define a community, or a group within a
community, as something unique in contra-distinction to its
neighbours. The elements of relativity, security and exclusivity deserve greater exploration, but it is intended to
concentrate the remainder of this paper on the element of
identity.

It is impossible here to review the number of contexts
in which the word identity is used, not to mention words
with similar implications such as 'knowing' or 'remembering'.
A few examples representing each of the way of life themes
must suffice however:

Personal Theme:
> "I like familiarity - too many new developments and
> changes make me feel alienated. I like a sense of
> belonging, of identity and continuity." (23)

> ". . . /

". . . remembering who you are, where you came from,
what has happened to you and your people. In a
country where so few outward things tell you that
you are Welsh it adds a quality of depth to the
consciousness . . ."(24)

Corporate Theme:
"the cultural identity of the people has been invaded
and their faith in the soundness of their way of
living impaired." (25)

"the (community) needs identifying points, which have
a long cycle of change, and by means of which things
changing on a shorter cycle can be valued and
identified." (26)

Cultural Theme:
". . . to conserve the language, thus maintaining the
cultural identity of the Shetlanders during a period
of social and economic transition." (27)

". . . cultural leadership with its stress on identity,
societal values, and national authenticity may, in
fact, be essential to the creation of a suitable climate
for worthwhile socio-economic progress . . ."(28)

Historical Theme:
"A community maintains itself, ensures a continuance
and an identity through such things as the shop, the
kirk . . . The place where the community lives is
important . . . in perpetuating its identity."(29)

"the most distressing part of this wholesale destruction
of dwellings . . . is that all knowledge is thus destroyed - all meaning of the generations who lived upon
this spot and went from here each day to hew coal . . ."(30)

Identity is thus used in two contexts, in an essentially
personal context, and in the context of a shared, communal
application. Personal identity has been defined as:

"the sense of feeling of being the same person,
based mainly on common sensibility and continuity
of aims, purposes and memories." (31)

and identity as:

"the character of persisting essentially unchanged."(32)

Identity is therefore something more than a mere label:
the/

the same label can very often denote two entirely different
phenomena (compare the label 'Bishop of Woolwich' as denoted
first by John Robinson and then by David Sheppard!). Instead
identity is essentially changeless and is based upon stimula-
tions experienced in an undifferentiated mass of sensations,
and upon a continuity of future, present and past. The oft-
expressed concerns of rural settlements, then, about the loss
of their identity in the fact of centralist policies, must
not be seen as something irrational, an unreasonable claim
for undeserved services, but rather as a product of the
totality of social processes both in time and through time.

> "Withdrawal, or a rundown of local services are a
> symbolic blow to the status of a small place.
> The closure of the secondary school or the railway
> station is one reason less for outsiders to have
> heard of the settlement. There is one less chance
> for the local people to project their image to
> outsiders . . . "(33)

Identity, furthermore, is not a commodity that can be taken
up at will, as a label might be. It is the product of a slow
maturing process, and can only be destroyed by dramatic
measures:

> ". . . if you can't believe in your past you're lost.
> If you went out of your way to undermine a community
> and demoralise it the best way you could possibly do
> it would be to cut it off from its own cultural back-
> ground, its history, its traditions and this is what
> has happened in the Highlands." (34)

And in Wales:

> "The loss of the language is the loss of an identity;
> it is the loss of a complete history and culture. . ."(35)

Many writers point to a trend in society towards the
retrieval of lost identities. On the personal level, Naomi
Mitchison states:

> "there/

> "there is a . . . crisis of identity . . . People
> do not really know who they are or why they are,
> and they have no continuity with past or future."(36)

and, more universally:

> "Even incomers are quick to see that things are done
> differently here, and are better for it. The (High-
> land) Region has important characteristics which
> must not be lost, they must be built upon and adapted
> to modern conditions."(37)

To lack identity is to be devoid of stimulation from society
and to be without an anchor in the passage of time. This
uprootedness:

> "is by far the most dangerous malady to which human
> societies are exposed, for it is a self-propagating
> one. For people who are really uprooted there remain
> only two possible sorts of behaviour: either to
> fall into a spiritual lethargy resembling death . . .
> or to hurl themselves into some form of activity. . .
> designed to uproot . . . those who are not yet up-
> rooted. . ."(38)

Identity is thus a concept important to society, and its
significance is ignored at our peril. The social scientists'
interpretation of the role of identity remains to be examined,
however, and from an apparently restricted literature one
study is reviewed.

In a comparative study of Newfoundland and Shetland,
Cohen argues that the encroachment of urban-inspired social
change produces conditions of marginality which then demand
that the local populace adopt new strategies of identity-
management(39). Cohen defines identity as:

> "a social process because . . . identity is always
> constructed by reference to others. The propagation
> of an identity is a presentation of self, designed
> in accordance with one's expectations of how others
> will react and respond; it is frequently informed
> by strategic attempts to evoke desired responses in
> others."(40)

The/

The social process of identity definition is described as:

> "The evaluation of a man's occupational performance
> and the very ideological status of his occupation
> (rebounding) upon the complex mesh of variables -
> kinship, religion, locality, prowess, character,
> allegiances, appearance and so on. . ."(41)

Cohen argues that attempts to define public identities take
two forms, 'assertive marginality' and 'assimilation' which:

> "comprise not just contrasting strategies but also
> contrasting ideologies of identity." (42)

In the former case the poor status afforded to the marginal
community is either dismissed as being externally imposed,
or is capitalised upon for the inherent positive values of
such a status. In the latter case customary local values
are deliberately abandoned in favour of the adoption of
those of the dominant culture. Through a detailed study
of Newfoundland and Shetland data which highlights the
strategies adopted in the management of identity, Cohen concludes that:

> "coping with marginality may be the greatest problem
> to follow in the wake of large-scale economic
> change."(43)

Thus, coping with marginality through the management of
identity in the wake of economic change may be seen as a
strictly sociological interpretation. However, it closely
parallels the processes already described, that is, the
coming to terms with relativities through the expression of
concern about identity in the face of social change, concern
often voiced in terms of way of life. This parallel clearly
needs further exploration, but the coincidence is sufficient
to suggest that any attempts to define way of life are both
intellectually possible and academically desirable, and
that the concept of identity may be the key.

N O T E S:

1. Stella Sutherland in the New Shetlander, 1974, 107, p.26.
2. S B Withey, "Values and Social Change" in OECD "Subjective elements of well-being" Vol 2, p21.
3. A Campbell, "Aspiration, satisfaction and fulfilment" in A Campbell and P Converse (eds.) "The Human meaning of social change" 1972, p441
4. ibid
5. Ulf Hannerz, "Soulside, Washington D C in the 1960's: Black Ghetto, culture and community" in C Bell and H Newby (eds.) "The sociology of community" 1974, p155.
6. Richard Hoggart, "The uses of literacy" 1957, p33.
7. E Mackinnon, "The Lion's Tongue" 1974, p98.
8. SDD, "Social consequences of oil developments" 1978, para 52.
9. J Wills, "The price of peace and quiet" in J Button (ed.) "The Shetland way of oil" 1978, p.35
10. Naomi Mitchison, "Oil for the Highlands" Fabian Research Series 315, 1974, p13.
11. ibid, p20.
12. Trevor Fishlock, "Wales and the Welsh" 1972, p107.
13. ibid, p184.
14. ibid, p11.
15. E Mackinnon, op cit, p104.
16. F G Vallee, "Social Structure and Organization in a Hebridean Community", unpublished PhD thesis, University of London, 1954, quoted in ibid, p87.
17. Neil Gunn, Lewis Grassic Gibbon, George Mackay Brown.
18. Emryn Jones quoted in HMSO "How do you want to live?" 1972, para 1.5.
19. ibid, para 2.29.
20. ibid, para 1.37.
21. Naomi Mitchison, "Solution to centralism and a world crisis of identity", The Scotsman, 6th April, 1970.

22./

22. R M MacIver, "The Ramparts We Guard", 1950, p87.

23. HMSO, op cit, para 3.4.

24. Ned Thomas, "The Welsh Extremist", 1971, p65.

25. Adam Collier, "The Crofting Problem",1953, p4.

26. S Woods quoted in G Bell and J Tyrwhitt (eds.),
    "Human identity in the urban environment" 1972,
    p383.

27. Tourism and Recreation Research Unit (University of
    Edinburgh), "Recreation in the Highlands and Islands"
    Research Report No 31, 1976, para 8.3.19.

28. Views of J A Fishman as in Mairtain O'Murchu, "Language
    and Community" Comhairle Na Gaeilge Occasional
    Paper No 1, 1970, Footnote 127, p43.

29. George Mackay Brown, "Seed, Dust, Star" in "Hawkfall"
    p105.

30. Charles Brister, "This is my Kingdom" 1972, p108.

31. Penguin Dictionary of Psychology.

32. ibid.

33. Adrian Varwell, "A Study of Industrial Settlements in a
    Sparsely Populated Area" unpublished PhD Thesis,
    University of Aberdeen, 1977, p144.

34. Iain Noble quoted in Derek Cooper "Hebridean Connection"
    1977, p65.

35. Saunders Lewis quoted in Trevor Fishlock, op cit, pp78, 79.

36. Naomi Mitchison, op cit.

37. Highland Regional Council, "Community Development in the
    Highland Region" 1978.

38. Simone Weil, "The Need for Roots, 1952, p45.

39. Anthony Cohen, "Social identity and the management of
    marginality", Institute for the Study of Sparsely
    Populated Areas (University of Aberdeen), "The
    Changing Fortunes of Marginal Regions" 1977,
    pp105-131.

40. ibid, p.107.

41. ibid, p.131.

42. ibid, p.109.

43. ibid, p.131.

SECTION   4

Self Image and Identity in the Hebrides
by Judith Ennew

The question of Hebridean identity and self image
might be resolved in academic enquiry, on the axis of
boundary maintenance, which has been much explored since
Barth's Ethnic Groups and Boundaries (Barth, 1969). Boundary
maintenance is particularly interesting in the case of
nomadic groups such as gypsies,   which continue to re-
establish a separate ethnic identity within a nation state
through manipulation of notions of cleanliness and unclean-
liness in order to maintain ideas of racial purity (Okely, 1975).
Identity is clearly a matter of 'ideas' rather than 'facts',
yet it relies upon the use, even manipulation of 'facts'.
This is why it presents a particularly difficult problem for
a social anthropology which increasingly focuses either on an
enclosed science of the mind, or upon the garnering and
analysis of factual material.

By concentrating upon the nebulous entity 'ideology',
this paper will inevitably appear unsubstantial. But a
consistent set of economic and political factors should be
retained as a backdrop. These are the factors which are
the central concern of the 'Way of Life' seminars and they
are related to the centralisation of political power and
administration and concomitant economic definition of
marginal areas as 'in need of development'. The dissatis-
faction of people in the marginal areas with the political
and economic 'solutions' to their 'problems' which have been
imposed or suggested by central government, were at the root
of the devolution debates of the 1970s. State policy in
the/

the twentieth century has attempted to industrialise these
marginal areas, to solve the problem of unemployment by
the creation of jobs. But by recognising these areas as
different, the State has also tended to bolster the notion
of distinct social entities that co-exist within a single
national polity.

In policy documents, as well as in the approach critic-
ised by Barth within social anthropology, it often appears
as if the boundaries to identity are clearly demarcated and
relatively stable. But for Barth, they are positioned and
maintained by identified and identifier in a generative
interaction and can be transcended. One does not wish to
deny that identity, 'What I Am', is given in 'What You Are
Not'. Yet both I and You vary according to context. The
islands of the Outer Hebrides are bounded geographically,
they present linguistic and cultural barriers to outsiders
and it may seem that these facts alone serve to explain
their feelings of differences; feelings strengthened through
looking inward and deciding upon a series of procedures, which
can be used to account for difference and maintain it in the
face of incursions from without. But the question is more
complex, for it involves not only people's statements about
what they are, but also their perception of what they are
told they are. And the boundary is not simply a single
generative structure but a set of interlocking ideas,
operating both internally and externally. The boundary is
in flux. It shifts according to context and it is in the
process of continuous historical construction, yet it
establishes in any one moment a strength of identity. The
strength of the barrier is amenable to immediate perception,
but its foundations are built on a quicksand of appearances.
It/

It leads towards the nebulous area of felt experience,
while deriving its <u>raison d'etre</u> from a series of concrete
facts which are appropriate to the moment in which it is
felt. In exploring this area, I make no apologies for
lapsing at times into unscientific incoherence. All that
I hope to show is that there are several interlocking
processes at work, in the maintenance of Hebridean identity
within the nation state and on a world stage where Hebrideans,
aware that they do not play their parts in isolation, cope
not only with speeches written for them but also with those
they write for themselves.

When teasing out this scenario, four principal constructs of identity emerge. All are dependent upon the
historical or actual existence of a pre-industrial, peasant
community. But the real existence of this entity is less
important than its existence in ideology or ideologies. The
first two constructs are those of the British State (to
which the EEC should be added) and of Academia. As will be
seen later, this is a closely related couple. I have
labelled the third construct 'Tourism', but it includes
elements of popular culture in novels, travelogues and media
representation. These are all externally-derived impressions,
but the fourth construct, while it draws upon the percepts
of the first two and images of the third, is the self-image
which Hebrideans construct for themselves. It has, above
all, a moral component, and alternates between two poles of
'good' and 'bad'. All four concepts are constructed around
ideas of difference, for the perception of identity only
occurs through a recognition of difference; between, for
example, here and there, then and now, self and other.
There/

There are therefore three aspects of identity always
present in perception of difference: spatial, temporal
and cognitive.

From the viewpoint of the State, the Hebridean identity
has been perceived as a problem since the nineteenth century.
Prior to this, the main difficulties envisaged by the body
politic were how to control and administer the area and how
best to colonise its resources. Through the process familiar
to students of Scottish history (kelp to sheep to oil) a
'redundant' population was produced. In the late nineteenth
century, changes in franchise altered the view of this
problem from redundancy to unemployment and the 'solution'
also changed from emigration to the provision of employment
in productive industry. For most of the twentieth century
the Hebrides has been regarded, implicitly or explicitly,
as under-developed. State policy has thus increasingly
identified the area through the existence of an unemployment
problem It has been defined as a region of difficulty,
marginal and poor in resources. The proposed solution is
to raise it to the level of the core of the nation state
through extending to it the benefits of growth economics
and a balanced economy. Thus the islands are described as
economically depressed and backward, relics of pre-industrial
society which need to be brought into the twentieth century.
The real problem, of course, is with the State rather than
the Hebrides. For, in addition to advocating growth and
industrialisation, the State acknowledges the different
identity of the region - its different 'way of life'.
Consequently it becomes committed simultaneously to growth
and to protection. The Hebrideans themselves are trapped
in this contradiction.

The/

The Academic construct of Hebridean identity works
on the idea of community in the genre of those community
studies which focus on the Celtic Fringe. From the Irish
Myth of Arensberg and Kimball (1940) to Fox's recent work
on the Tory Islanders (1979), the twilight of Celtic areas
is illuminated by a series of contrasting dichotomies.
Malcolm Chapman's book The Gaelic Vision in Scottish Culture
(1978) explores these oppositions in literature and sociology.
He shown how pairs of contrasts like Celt versus Anglo Saxon,
are strengthened by oppositions such as mechanical versus
organic solidarity, even female versus male in the development of academic ideas about Celtic regions. Moreover,
he notes revealingly that the difficulty of finding a secure
Gaelic identity is analogous to that experienced by feminism
in delineating a female role which is not prescribed by a
'patriarchal' society.

Academic sociology and anthropology in general have
provided a ratification of State policy in 'remote rural
areas' by developing the apparent contradiction between
State and community; they have 'tribalised Europe' by
concentrating upon the village as an isolated entity.
Communities thus conceived have been studied as isolated from
control, with the consequent elaboration of the role of the
'broker'. With the addition of a tradition versus modernity
axis, they are studied in isolation from history. Kinship
is the focus of concern; the 'criss-crossing ties' described
by Arensberg and Kimball are seen as the basis of a moral
community and of a peasant conservatism which is resistant
to change. In addition, communities are studied as isolated
from economic growth. Their resources are 'poor', they have
a natural inability to grow.

Academic/

Academic statements on the Hebrides are relatively
rare. In one of the earliest, Geddes suggests that the
area presents a pre-industrial model of moral advantage
for the rest of the nation. He stresses the advantages
of communal life and unchanging tradition, but this results in him treating the Hebridean as a fossilised artefact. Some idea of the flavour of his work can be gained
from the following quotation:

> "In the 'Outer Hebrides', commonly regarded as
> the most 'outlying' inhabited lands of the
> British Isles, are revealed not only the most
> ancient of British rocks, but probably the oldest
> form of communal life in Britain. This life, in
> present and past, will interest some by character-
> istics which may seem unique. But it will interest
> others by features of underlying universality.
> These might be compared to the Archaean rock,
> overlain towards the south-east by a succession of
> younger strata, but forming their foundation."
> (Geddes, 1955, pp3-4).

It can be seen that this is not an out-dated attitude in
anthropology in Fox's work on the Tory Islanders whom he
offers to academic study in one place as 'living fossils'
(Fox, 1979, p122) and in another as suitable objects for
experiment (ibid, p125).

In similar fashion, a study made of Barra for a PhD
thesis in 1954 amounted to an evaluation of community
ethos in the face of gradually intruding industrial
technology (Vallee, 1954). More recently and more usefully
the description of social change in Susan Parman's doctoral
thesis concentrates upon ideas of boundedness derived from
Barth. She concludes that there is a strong sense of
boundedness in Shawbost, a village on the West coast of
Lewis, because of the constraints and incentives of wider
British society. According to her analysis, villagers are
not/

not necessarily trying to maintain a static tradition but
economising in the face of incursive State practices
(Parman, 1971).

Outside the limits of social anthropology, human
geography and economics define the Hebrides as a backward
peripheral region characterised by poor resources. The
HIDB uses this approach which treats the difference between
marginal area and industrial core as a 'natural' geographical
occurrence, a definition which is self-perpetuating but not
without its ambiguities (cf Kay, 1975, pp6-7). Both State
and Academic pronouncements are based upon an apparent
collection of factual data, the labels they apply to the
Hebridean thus gain an additional strength or authenticity
in the production of internal and external stereotypes.
By delineating both 'problem' and 'sense of community' for
the islanders they not only produce the reasons for a
particular state of affairs they also produce the precon-
ditions under which that situation is experienced.

In contrast to the problems provided within these two
constructs, the Tourist nexus relies upon an image of a
solution which is integrated with the community ethos of the
academic view. From intellectual tourists like Pennant,
Boswell and Johnson in the eighteenth century, through the
Balmoralism of the nineteenth, the Hebrideans were regarded
as the 'wild men of Europe'. In twentieth-century media and
for tourists now, they represent a refuge of peace, quiet
and tranquillity; and available image to contrast with notions
or urban stress. To the romantic imagination, fostered by
summer visitors and tourist agencies, there is no Hebridean
Problem and the contrast operating between here (urban areas
of the UK) and there (the Highlands and Hebrides) are:
the/

the Rat Race _versus_ the Good Life, the present _versus_ the
past and the pedantic _versus_ the romantic. There are elements
of this in conservationist lobbies which were particularly
noticeable in the early stages of the oil boom. The preser-
vation of scenery and a way of life in this context often
takes on a proto-museum approach. Once again the native
Hebridean appears as an artefact. Acceptance of the notion
that 'we have something special up here' is common. It is
an image played out for summer visitors and strongly drawn
upon for the benefit of both academic investigators and
'white settlers', without usually being verbalised in anything
other than general terms. Yet there is a contradiction in this
construct also. It could be seen when the British subsidiary
of a Norwegian company applied for planning permission to
build an oil-related development at Arnish in Lewis. The
local authority received one objection on the grounds of the
scenic beauty of the proposed site from a 'white settler' who
lived on the other side of the island. But a petition in
favour of the proposal, because of the employment prospects
it offered, was signed by 21 Lewismen, most of whom would
normally shrink from making such a public statement.

The Tourist construct not only fails to recognise this
sort of contradiction, but also fatally ignores the obvious
stresses of island life in an attempt to promulgate a vision
of the perfection of rural, peasant life. It does not admit
to knowledge of the available statistics regarding two pre-
vailing island enigmas: alcoholism and clinical depression.
The drink problem in particular is not allowed to intrude
in the literature without fierce opposition from the Hebrideans
themselves. In 1949, Alisdair Alpin MacGregor published a
book/

book <u>The Western Isles</u> which included a savage attack on
the islanders' morals and values, particularly drinking
habits, and suggested that the people were idle and an
unnecessary burden on the taxpayer (MacGregor, 1949, p350).
MacGregor had previously written widely on the subject of
the Hebrides (where he claimed ancestry) producing many
glowing accounts of the remote and misty islands. The
response to this new book was swift. The Lewis Association,
a group of local observers and political lobbyists, devoted
an entire Report to 'countering the attack on the good name
of the people of the Hebrides' (Lewis Association Report No 6
p5). The Association report attacked MacGregor's personality,
accused him of making factual errors and finally presented a
'True Picture' of Lewis people: 'they are peasants; they
are descended from warriors and sea-rovers; they are separated
from the ways of living of the cities by mountains and a waste
of seas' (ibid p34).

The spatial separation involved here as part of the self-
image is important. But all the images referred to above
are present in some form in island thought. Moreover it
should not be forgotten that there are differences <u>between</u>
islanders which dictate which aspects of those images are
dominant in any individual identity. In Lewis, in particular,
the distinction between Christian and non-Christian is clearly
drawn, in dress and modes of behaviour which operate well
outside the confines of the purely religious ritual of taking
communion in the Free Church, on which the distinction is
based. There are, of course, intergenerational differences
in perception of and identification with external national
components. In Lewis there is also a felt distinction between
Stornowegians and the 'Maoris' who live in landward areas and
this/

this is partly related to the major difference between
bilingual Gaelic/English speakers and Gaelic monoglots.

In the interaction between the first and the last of
these intra-island differences is the core of a fundamental
contradiction which cuts across the simple dichotomies which
have appeared until now in this paper. It may seem that the
connection between the strictly Puritan churches of Lewis
and the Gaelic language is strong. The dogma of the Free
Church is that the Hebrides are the last bastion of Christian-
ity in a misguided or heretical world. It has appropriated
formal archaic Gaelic as a medium of worship and developed a
specific sung form of Gaelic psalmody. The church regulates
the cultural life of Lewis and it is the forces of such
bodies as the Lord's Day Observance Society which are active
in challenging forces of modernity such as the oil industry
which threaten the 'way of life' of the island; for in such
cases the 'way of life' is synonymous with some religious
ideal.

It has been suggested that Hebrideans are not only bilingual but also bicultural, that the social problems of the
area derive from a conflict between two sets of norms which
are bounded on the one side by the Church/Gaelic complex and
on the other by secularisation and English (Thomson 1974 p265).
But it is also important to remember that only one type of
Gaelic has been appropriated by the church and that the
language retains, in its everyday form of 'peasant patois'
(McKinnon, 1971 p20), elements of an earlier mysticism, even
animism. These elements do not co-exist in total harmony
with the precepts of Puritanism. Thus if one analyses the
obituaries in the <u>Stornoway Gazette</u> (and where better to
seek the features of an ideal type than in this particular
written/

written form?) not one, but two sets of Gaelic values
emerge. The true Christians of the Church are eulogised
for their upright spirituality, their attributes of God-
given grace. On the other hand, the company of 'nature's
gentlemen' appears as an alternative ideal, granted the
attribute of wit which is essentially manifested in the
Gaelic language. Thus Hebrideans are not bicultural but
tricultural. Besides the contrast between inside and outside,
between Gaelic culture and English sophistication, there is
a further distinction to be drawn between, in the words of one
Lewisman, Gaelic mysticism and Puritan rationality (Ennew,
1980).

The interplay between these two internal normative
systems is one element in the demoralisation and disorientation
which are at the basis of social problems such as alcoholism
and clinical depression. I would suggest that this complex
also fundamentally affects attitudes towards economic
development, that 'backwardness' is due to a confusion of
identity rather than to some identification with peasant conservatism and tradition. When one studies the economic
and social history of the Hebrides one is struck by the
inevitable development of feelings of scorn and despair
directed at government policies and industrial enterprises.
This is the result of the often inconsistent and contradictory identities and solutions offered by State and Academic
constructs. But there is also an uncomfortable feeling that
at some point a self-fulfilling prophecy of failure arose.

As Hebridean identity swings between poles of 'good'
and 'bad' images, one frequently hears the implicit or
explicit statement that 'nothing good can ever happen here'.
Extraordinary/

Extraordinary pride is shown in the achievements of
permanent migrants. Every family can tell the life history
of some brother or cousin who is 'making a fortune' as a
doctor or lawyer in Mainland Scotland or England. It is
often recalled that MacAulay was of Lewis descent. But
these glories do not reflect back on those who are left
behind, except with some kind of negative regret. And this
can take the form of fierce recrimination against local
innovators which is only partly explained by notions such
as conservatism or the Limited Good hypothesis. Thus the
recently formed Gaelic Theatre Company <u>Fir Chlis</u> (Northern
Lights) received better reviews of its productions in
<u>The Guardian</u> than in the <u>Stornoway Gazette</u>.

   The insecurity of identity is also evident in hyper-
sensitivity to external criticism. This is partly the
result of clinging to the 'good' image of Academic and
Tourist constructs; the moral superiority of the peasant
community. Perception of external criticism is heightened
to an extraordinary degree, so that the essentially sympathetic
treatment given to the 'Gaelic vision' by Malcolm Chapman
is not only misunderstood, but the author is accused of
'paranoia' and racial bias (MacNeacail in <u>West Highland
Free Press</u>, January 1978). Thus while the virtues of the
Hebridean identity are strongly asserted, there is a
simultaneous tendency to overstress the position of economic
and political disadvantage. Let me hasten to add that I
would not wish to deny for one moment that the history of
the Hebrides is one of progressive de-development. That is
in the realm of 'fact'. But at the level of idea or ideology
there is an oral tradition amounting to mythology in its
anxious repetition, one which justifies all present ills in
terms/

terms of past dispossessions. Thus almost every enquiry made by a social researcher is answered in the first instance by reference to oral traditions of Clearances and emigrations. These, and not the half-forgotten tales collected by folk-lorists for insertion in an academic version of Tourist constructs, are the authentic myths of the Hebrides.

Finally one should consider the present conscious efforts to establish a secure identity based partly on the recuper-ation by Hebrideans of their own history. This has been taken on as a task by a number of mature, qualified returners who are involved in a series of varied projects ranging from the Gaelic Theatre Company to the Schools Bilingual Project. Language undoubtedly plays a major role in this, for the case for Gaelic is simultaneously a case for identity. The number of such projects and their apparently spontaneous appearance at roughly the same point in time, seem to denote some major trend towards reconstruction. But, for the moment, to have a Hebridean identity is to be part of a self-contradictory, shifting, internally inconsistent set of ideological con-structs which are only partially 'indigenous'. The contrasts outlined above can all be regarded as false dichotomies. The Hebridean identity is the product of a continuing historical relation rather than of a continuous historical difference. Perception of difference at any one moment is a product of this relationship.

N O T E:

This paper was first presented at the SSRC 'Way of Life' seminar in May 1979. A revised version has appeared in Cambridge Anthropology Volume 6, Nos. 1 and 2 (Special issue on European Ethnography). The present version contains further revisions.

Bibliography/

BIBLIOGRAPHY

Arensberg C and Kimball S, 1940 <u>Family and Kinship in Ireland</u>; Peter Smith

Barth F, 1969 <u>Ethnic Groups and Boundaries</u>; George Allen & Unwin.

Chapman M, 1978 <u>The Gaelic Vision in Scottish Culture</u>; Croom Helm.

Ennew J, 1980 <u>The Western Isles Today</u>; Cambridge University Press.

Fox R, 1979 <u>The Tory Islanders</u>; Cambridge University Press.

Geddes A, 1955 <u>The Isle of Lewis and Harris</u>: Edinburgh University Press.

Kay G, 1975 <u>Development and Underdevelopment</u>; Macmillan.

MacGregor A A, 1949 <u>The Western Isles</u>; Robert Hale Ltd.

McKinnon K, 1971 A sociological study of Scottish Gaelic, MA Thesis, London.

Okely J, 1975 Gypsy Women: models in conflict in Arnener A S (ed.) <u>Perceiving Women</u>; Malaby Press.

Parman S, 1972 Sociocultural change in a Scottish crofting township; PhD Thesis, Rice University, Texas.

Thomson D, 1974 <u>An Introduction to Gaelic Poetry</u>; Victor Gollanz.

Vallee F, 1954 Social structure and agriculture in a Hebridean Community; PhD Thesis, London.

Gala Day as an Expression of Community Identity
by Robert Turner

The concept of identity, when applied to people, can
be formulated on several levels, dependent on context.
Crudely speaking, we may talk of individual identity,
though there is a considerable degree of interaction
between these various identities. It can be argued that
individual identity presupposes the existence of an
identifiable community, which generates a cultural language,
or code, rendering individual expressions of identity
meaningful.

'Family identity', in the town to be discussed here,
represents a primary level of categorization within the
community. The question 'who is he/she?' commonly requires
an answer framed in kinship terms, where the unknown person's
relationship is traced either to one of the interlocutors
or to a mutually well-known local figure. By this means
someone is 'placed'; if this turns out to be impossible,
he is classified as a 'stranger' and is assigned a different
set of expectations.

'Community identity' can be described as a bundle of
norms and expectations which are seen as <u>specific</u> to the
town, Cockenzie and Port Seton, and which are regarded as
continuing and permanent within this community. Aspects of
community identity are made explicit in any collective
local event, ranging from church services to darts competitions - but finds its fullest expression, in the view
of the author, in the annual Gala Day ceremonies.

These/

These proceedings, which Bernardo Bernardi would describe as a form of 'popular religion', attract large enthusiastic crowds, and can safely be said to represent the only occasion in which the majority of the local population participates. Gala Day is a classic example of 'secular ritual', as analysed by Moore and Myerhoff (Introduction to Secular Ritual, eds. S F Moore and B G Myerhoff, 1977, Asses: Van Gorcum). They distinguish five ways of looking at the outcome of secular ritual, which can all be identified in the description of Gala Day given here. These are:

(1) Explicit purpose - "the manifest meaning, the simplest to understand, and often likely to be the most super- ficial.

(2) Explicit symbols and messages - "a ceremony activates or presents selected ideas necessarily related to larger cultural frameworks of thought and explanation . . . It may also make available many symbolic elements which are fragmentary, separate, and evidently unsystematized."

(3) Implicit statements - "a ceremony . . . may be an act of affirmation, a declaration of structural strength, a presentation of apparent certainties, continuity, and the like."

(4) Social relationships affected - "there may be effects on the participants which directly involve their social roles, identities, sense of collective contact, attitudes to other persons . . ."

(5) Culture versus chaos - "at its most general level, all collective ceremony can be interpreted as a cultural statement about cultural order as against a cultural void." (All quotes from Moore and Myerhoff, p16).

Many/

Many towns in the East of Scotland have similar Gala
Days, but a comparative study is still awaited. There is a
suggestion[1] that a primary classification may be made between
those which are rigidly scripted and those which are re-
devised each year and endeavour to include topical elements.
The 'Seton Queen Celebrations' to be described here are un-
equivocally scripted. Several informants assert that the
order of events, and even the wording of the speeches, have
remained unchanged for thirty years.

A short account of the sequence of events will be made,
followed by analysis in detail of some of the events, with
emphasis on features affirming community identity. Finally
the historical development and practical logistics of the
ceremony will be described, which will demonstrate the claims
of Gala Day to be seen as the prime expression of this
identity.

A programme published by the Gala Day Committee (the
events organizing body) is sold from door to door a few days
beforehand. It gives the following order of events:

11.45 a.m.	Assembly at the Green
	Laying of wreaths at the
	War Memorial
	Procession to the West Harbour
12.00 noon	Embarkation for Port Seton
	Procession from West to East Harbour
12.30 p.m.	Arrival of Royal Party at Port Seton
	Reception by Chairman
	Procession to Public Park
1.30 p.m.	CROWNING CEREMONY
	Queen's Champion delivers the
	Challenge
	Maids of Honour prepare the Queen
	Elect for the Crowning Ceremony
	Queen/

---

1. The author would like to thank Adrian Varwell for
this suggestion.

> Queen Pauline is crowned
> Sceptre Bearer gives Sceptre to
>   the Ex-Queen, who delivers it to
>   Queen Pauline
> Herald reads the Royal Proclamation
> Presentation of characters to
>   Queen Pauline
> Presentation to the Dux of the school
> Presentation of model barge to the
>   Queen
> Parade of Fancy Dress Competitors
> Votes of thanks - Mrs. G. Watson
> Entertainment and tea.

The main actors throughout are children at Cockenzie
Primary School. However, the Programme states explicitly
that Gala Day is not a school activity, and school staff are
not present in their official capacity. Nonetheless, several
teachers were observed co-ordinating the events, and prepar-
ations and rehearsals are all carried out in the school.
Normally the school deliberately discourages involvement of
parents in educational activities, so it is probable that
this disclaimer is an attempt to defuse any suggestion of
exclusivity, a temporary lowering of the social barrier between
the school and the public, in the interests of universality.

(1) Assembly at the Green

This Green was presented to the local fishermen by
the lairds, the Cadells, in the nineteenth century, as a place
to dry their nets. It is just across the road from the
Cadells' former mansion, and has never been seen as a place
for children to play. It is a formal, almost sacred, public
space, and was the natural site for the erection of a War
Memorial after the Great War. On Gala Day, exceptionally,
a large crowd of adults and children gathers there, waiting
for the arrival of the Queen-elect and her entourage, and
admiring the costumes of those children taking part in the
fancy/

fancy dress competition (who are not included in the
Queen-elect's party). Eventually, preceded by a marching
pipe band from the nearest colliery, the Queen-elect's float
arrives, together with a few other decorated floats con-
taining costumed children.

(2) Laying of wreaths at the War Memorial

It is significant that this is the first formal event
of the Day, inviting comparison with sacrifices made to
ancestor spirits in certain Bantu societies. It is a very
solemn part of the proceedings, made more so by the fact
that it is not the Queen-elect, elected by the popular vote
of the two eldest (Primary Seven) classes at the Primary
School, but the Dux of the School, as selected by the
'professional' school teachers, who actually lays the wreath.
Both in some sense represent the community, but the Dux of
the School (in 1978 the daughter of a Community Councillor)
is chosen by what are regarded as more objective and absolute
criteria to perform this supreme honour and duty. Education,
we are given to understand, is of greater value than mere
popularity. Patriotism is a highly regarded aspect of
community identity; it has to be the finest flower of the
community's children that lays the wreath. Curiously enough,
this does not seem to form part of Gala Day ceremonies elsewhere in East Lothian, and is not mentioned in local news-
paper reports of the Day. The other occasion on which wreaths
are laid at the War Memorial is the Armistice Day service in
November; the only time, until recent years, when both
local Churches of Scotland willingly conducted a United
Service. The Gala Day wreath-laying evokes this 'universal',
schism-denying, aspect of local identity.

(3)/

(3) Procession to the West Harbour

The general clockwise movement of the proceedings
around the village is consistent with the widespread con-
viction among Scottish fishing communities that it is
auspicious to 'turn with the Sun'. The subsequent progress
from the Old Harbour (West Harbour) to the New Harbour (East
Harbour) reflects the long-term movement of the social and
economic centre of the community from the vicinity of
Cockenzie House to the commercial nucleus around the New
Harbour, open in 1880, and now the harbour mainly used by
the fishing boats. Fishing boats never enter the Old Harbour
now, except on Gala Day, unless they need repair at the
boatyard there. The procession now splits into two sections.

(4) Embarkation for Port Seton

The Queen-elect and her escort are taken on board a
number of fishing boats, specially painted and decorated
with bunting for the occasion, and led by a 'Royal Barge'
chosen previously by lottery to transport the Queen-elect.
More than half the boats registered in Port Seton, including
(at great expense) a few large boats normally stationed in
Eyemouth or North Shields, assemble on the morning of Gala
Day in Port Seton Harbour, where they are lined up with
unusual neatness. On cue, they come into the Old Harbour
in Cockenzie by ones and twos, and each takes on board as many
as 50 children and adults from the Gala Day procession -
usually related in various ways to crew members. A number of
small boys have been previously dressed up as pirates or
sailors - boats carrying 'pirates' display the 'Jolly Roger'
and those with 'sailors', the Royal Ensign.

During the voyage, which lasts 30-45 minutes, the boats
zoom round and round each other, in a series of intricate
manoeuvres. One year there was a serious collision resulting
in/

in fights between fishermen. 'Very' flares are let off -
the idea is to give a symbolic impression of a sea battle
between the Queen-elect's Escort boats and the Pirate boats,
which are normally equal in numbers. The result of the mock
battle, which is always the same, is that the 'pirates' are
defeated and captured by the Queen-elect's sailors; later
they are freed when they promise to contribute to the subsequent 'revels', and to be loyal subjects of the Queen.

These events may be interpreted as expressing further
aspects of community identity. The Queen-elect, undergoing a
sort of initiation ordeal, is carried on a fishing boat,
which reflects the traditional economic dependence of the
town on the success of the fishing industry. It is highly
significant that under normal circumstances it is seen as
very unlucky to have a woman on a boat at sea. Gala Day,
asserting community identity, cuts across the binary oppositions
male : female :: boats : houses - though it is striking that
the fishing boats are re-categorised as state or fighting vessels
for the occasion. Again the theme of patriotism is stressed,
though the magnanimity shown to the defeated 'pirates' suggests
that chauvinism is not approved.

(5) <u>Procession from West to East Harbours</u>

While this drama is taking place at sea, the rest of the
crowd makes its way down the old High Street from one harbour
to the other. This evokes the Fishermen's Walk which took
place on the now defunct Box Meeting Day (of which, more later),
when fishermen and their womenfolk danced in the streets in
front of each pub, making a full clockwise circuit of the
High Street and Edinburgh Road, including a stop at the Holy
Well. Cultural continuity is expressed in this activity,
linking former and present custom.

(6)/

(6) Crowning Ceremony

The complexity and symbolic richness of this ceremony cannot be briefly summarised, and only a few comments are presented here.

The crowd gathered in the public Park, in the newest part of Port Seton, numbers in thousands. The atmosphere is cheerful and playful; ladies from the Church Guilds sell tea and biscuits from small marquees, and the town's ubiquitous caterers, Di Ciacca's, sell icecream as they have at local public events for the last fifty years. This is a voluntaristic celebration of community identity, rather than a pious enactment of moral norms as would be found in the now extinct ritual of Kirkin' the Council. All the actions are established by tradition - there is no room for character acting, reference to topical events, or self-mockery.

The crowning itself is performed by a well-known and well-respected local lady - the wife of the District Councillor, or of the headmaster or doctor, or of a successful local business-man. It was commonly done by the Provost's wife, before local government reorganization. There is no evidence that any one lady ever performed the crowning twice - like the Queen, one could only be crowner once. Two points should be made about this: firstly, the choice of a prestigious local lady as crowner confers, but only indirectly, 'civic' legitimacy on the proceedings. Gala Day is not seen as a serious enough occasion to warrant the pomp and dignity of a male notable, such as the Provost, performing the Crowning. The choice of a lady was explained by one informant, however, on the grounds that 'they did it more gracefully' - the idea of a man doing it seemed 'awful strange'. Secondly, the sharing around of the task of crowning the Queen prevents its possible use by any/

any particular lady as a means of increasing her prestige, which would be seen as divisive in this tenaciously egalitarian community.

The only non-preordained part of the Crowning Ceremony script comes right at the beginning, and it is not mentioned in the Programme. This consists of the 'Jester' reading out the names of the winners of the fancy dress competition, as a prologue or preamble to the crowning ceremony proper. The 'Jester' is a small boy dressed in fool's garb and his voice is scarcely audible - it seems entirely appropriate that he should be responsible for the only contingent part of the proceedings. Nevertheless, the fancy dress competition is the focus of a great deal of energy, money, and enthusiasm; 30 or 40 children take part. Clearly, it is deliberately subordinated to the formal events of the day - this effectively symbolizes the superordination of integrative, unitive moral values on this great occasion. Traditionally, Scottish fishing villages foster a very powerful degree of competitiveness, perhaps because each individual has a wide network of significant others. But wisely, it is laid down in the Gala Day that the costumes of the leading figures are fixed, frequently stored and passed on each year. The focal personages cannot be used as an arena for inter-household competition.

The 'Royal Proclamation' is read out by the Herald(a small boy), and summarizes economically many features of the idealized community identity expressed in Gala Day. The fact that it is printed in full in the Programme demonstrates how seriously it is to be taken; the text will be quoted in full:

> Whereas it has come to our knowledge that many of
> our faithful and devoted subjects desire to know our
> royal mind concerning divers important questions, we
> do desire that our royal will and pleasure be set
> forth and made known in the following proclamation:

That/

That our loyal subjects strive to live in peace,
charity and goodwill, one towards the other;

That the spirit of purity in word, thought and
action be cultivated;

That a respectful and ready obedience be given to
all parents, teachers and those placed in authority;

That diligent and careful attention be given to
those things taught at school and to the lessons
to be learned from Nature;

That a spirit of reverence be fostered for the
power and goodness of the Great and Wise Creator.

It is our royal command that these great traditions
of our realm be upheld by all our loyal subjects
throughout the ensuing year.

Given at our Court, at Port Seton, this 17th day
of June, in the year of our Lord, one thousand,
nine hundred and seventy-eight

Pauline - Queen

This proclamation, which could be described as a sort
of local 'Ten Commandments', will not be discussed at length.
There is an interesting progression from the personal to the
abstract, commencing with interpersonal relations and ending
with relationship with God - with the effect of placing stress
on each of these.

Following the proclamation, 'Characters' - children in
symbolic dress - are presented to the Queen, as her subjects.
Their order is interesting. First is Britannia, the most
inclusive category, with shield and trident. Then Scotland,
England, Ireland and Wales - evidently in diminishing order of
local importance. Next the seasons, in correct temporal order:
Spring, Summer, Autumn, Winter - there is an exceptional emphasis
on weather as a topic of conversation in Cockenzie (presumably
related to fishing, ultimately). Then a girl dressed as 'The
Spirit/

Spirit of Goodwill' - the only virtue personified in this
entire pageant, and thus picked out as the most important
(as we have already seen in the Royal Proclamation). This
too is not surprising in a community where malicious gossip
is endemic (a powerful means of social control), and is
universally condemned even by its chief practitioners.

Next come two 'Fisher Girls' dressed in traditional
padded skirts and striped petticoats, with creels on their
backs - a reminder of the relative economic independence of
women in this village when their menfolk were away at the
herring for 6 or 7 months of each year. Even during the
winter when men fished local waters for white fish, women
formed an indispensable part of the domestic mode of production,
preparing the tackle and marketing the catch. It is worth
pointing out that while males are involved in the Gala Day
proceedings (by contrast with the all-female 'Gang Show',
another extremely popular event), they always play a merely
supportive role - crewing the boats, speaking on the Queen's
behalf etc. Yet local economic, political and religious
authority are now firmly in men's hands. It could thus be
argued that Gala Day includes an element of ritual role-
reversal (cf. M Gluckman, Custom and Conflict in Africa,
Chapter V). The idea of female church elders, let alone
female ministers, is anathema to most of the local population,
and female Town Councillors were most unusual.

Returning to the pageant, next come girls dressed in
national costume of seven nations: China, USA, Holland, Spain,
Jamaica, Thailand and India. No attempt is made to use actual
representatives of these nations, which are selected mainly
because they have distinctive and attractive national dress.
The/

The sequence appears to be arbitrary; but the message is
that at least ideologically, Cockenzie is superior to anywhere else in the world. Informants have commented seriously
that they regard Cockenzie as the best place in the world to
live; the District Councillor, without any irony, has named his
house 'Shangri-La'.

(7) Votes of Thanks

After the Crowning Ceremony, the Chairman of the Gala
Day Committee, Mrs. G. Watson (or 'Chrissie Yowe', as she is
usually known) gives a vote of thanks to the various groups
and individuals who helped with the proceedings. These are
the traditional groups: the fishermen, the church women's
guilds, the school, the local shopkeepers. The workers at the
nearby power station opened in 1968 are not included. Mrs.
Watson has the right background for her central role; she comes
from a family which can trace its Cockenzie descent for more
than six generations and which included one of the founders
of Gala Day. Her husband works for the District Council
(albeit at a 'skilled manual' level).

Finally, the Queen and her Court leave the stage, and
the rest of the day is given over to competitive sports
activities, and, in the evening, a Gala Day Ball for the
adults.

A penumbra of other activities surrounds Gala Day. These
are mainly competitive. There is a competition for the 'best-
dressed house', where households decorate the outside of their
houses with crêpe paper and flags in a tacitly-agreed style,
and a small committee of judges award prizes. Most involved
in this competition are the houses where members of the Queen's
retinue live - competition is sometimes quite keen. Further
competitions include 'best-dressed shop window' and 'best-
dressed boat'. In these we see a formal recogntion and a
channelling/

channelling into socially acceptable forms of the pervasive urge to compete, made, again, firmly subordinate to the uncompetitive, consensual, rubrical core of Gala Day.

We pass on to the history and logistics of the Day. In about 1880, a Fisherman's Friendly Society was established in Cockenzie. Such foundations were frequent at that time. The contributions and documents were stored, in the care of the secretary/treasurer of the society, the local schoolmaster, in a large padlocked Box. This Box was publicly opened annually in September for the disbursements of benefits to those eligible by reason of sickness, widowhood, etc. This day became a local holiday and festival, known as Box Meeting Day, and served as the occasion for much merry-making; weddings, dancing in the streets, ceremonial burning of old boats. Its timing was determined by the annual herring fishing cycle, which started in April off the Hebrides and came round clockwise to Yarmouth in December. Box Meeting Day was primarily an adult occasion, a Saturnalia when the normal standards of behaviour, hard-working, puritanically-religious, were laid aside.

However, as time went by values changed, fishermen prospered, and by 1950 Box Meeting Day had become merely another opportunity to get extremely drunk. Respectable young women, who used to dress up in beautiful white smocks for the occasion, started to stay at home - the event had lost its innocence and charm. Furthermore, fishing had lost much of its economic importance to the community and seemed at that time to be dying out. The funds of the Fishermen's Friendly Society had become negligible by comparison with Welfare State Benefits, partly owing to the fishermen's economic naïveté.

It was in this climate that in 1946 a local Provost and school headmaster, originally from a neighbouring mining village/

village, introduced the idea of holding a Gala Day each year,
after the long established tradition of Miner's Galas. A
group of men and women formed the first Gala Day Committee.
The included the Provost, Mr M; the manager of the ships
chandlery, Mr H, who was also a playwright, organist and
amateur film-maker; a builder and powerful Freemason, Mr O;
and members of the women's branch of the local Labour Club, in
particular a charismatic lady in the same family as the present
chairman.

Together, these local worthies devised, or choreographed,
the ceremonies of Gala Day, from diverse sources. Mr H contri-
buted the idea of putting the Gala Queen to sea in a fishing
boat. Mr M used experience from his native mining village to
devise the crowning ceremony itself. Mr O provided the Herald's
speech, taken from his own schooldays. The very title 'Seton
Queen' came from the nickname given to Mrs O's grandmother, a
formidable lady in her time. Even the Queen's robe had to be
borrowed from the Gala wardrobe of a neighbouring village for
the first two years.

But, by all accounts, the first Gala Day was a resounding
success. Those who had devised it had obviously struck a chord
with the local community, providing a suitable vehicle for
expression of community identity. By the late 1950's Gala Day
had become a great occasion; ostentation grew to remarkable
heights. The Queen's retinue wore what amounted to wedding
dresses, and were transported in carriages. The crowner was
expected to donate a gold watch to the Queen after the ceremony. Eventually escalation became prohibitively expensive
and things were toned down a bit; a tacit agreement was
reached that enough was enough. This competitive display was
<u>always</u> restricted to incidentals, however, and was never
allowed to enter the core of the ceremony.

By/

By 1960 the Gala Day had taken over from Box Meeting
Day, according to several informants. The latter survived
only a few more years. How can we explain this? It appears
that the concept of <u>community identity</u> offers a useful
starting point. Historically, Cockenzie was a traditional
fishing village in 1900, but developed into a mixed economy,
in which mining played an increasingly important role, by 1950.
Politically, the village had changed from a semi-autonomous
burgh under the benign paternalism of the local Whig Laird,
to a more republican, proletarian burgh, where the Town Council
(made up of local burgesses) owned most of the houses and maintained the town's cultural integrity using the powerful means
of council house allocation. Most of the functions of the
Fishermen's Friendly Society had been taken over by the Welfare
State, fishermen finding themselves in an exceptionally favour-
able position as regards taxation and unemployment insurance.
The dominant ideology had also changed, from a traditionalistic,
paternalistic idealism to an economic rationalism with little
scope for expression of community solidarity.

Thus it makes sense that the old ceremony lapsed and the
new came into vogue: the old could not adapt, tied as it was
to its increasingly irrelevant economic role, while the new
was custom-made to express the changed community identity.
As Cockenzie became less 'traditional', with the influx of
miners, increased mobility and the decline of fishing, it became increasingly self-conscious about its traditions and
sought to perpetuate them in a highly stylized form: Gala
Day.

One element of community identity plays little part in
the proceedings: religion. Though church attendance is high,
it is divided among a number of different churches and sects.
This/

This may perhaps explain why the only reference to religion
in the ceremonies is vague and unspecific; anything more
explicit might be seen to be <u>divisive</u>, favouring one denomi-
nation rather than the others. Similarly, Box Meeting Day
had little explicit religious content.

To summarize, Gala Day can be seen as an event indigenously
constructed, as a <u>bricolage</u>, from various elements already
present in local culture, in such a way as to provide an
occasion for expression of an idealised collective identity.
Annually, it reasserts an acceptable definition of the
situation, and acts as an opportunity for extensive co-operation
between different sectors of the population not usually so
linked. While it permits competitive display, it makes such
display clearly subordinate to the integrative core of the
ceremony which is an atavistic recollection of a monarchical
city-state. How well it succeeds as a celebration of
community identity is attested by its immense popularity.

SECTION   6

Discussion

The above papers are revised versions of those originally
presented at the Second Way of Life Seminar. However, not all
the papers that were read are included here because they were
essentially 'work in progress' reports and some are not yet
ready for publication. As in most seminars the main object is
to discuss the papers presented and this concluding section will
mention the exchanges which are relevant to these particular
published papers, besides attempting some generalizations.

1.   Regarding Jackson's postulated assertion that stereotypes
were used about 'strangers only' did not this overlook the fact
that stereotypes were often used in arguments between members of
a community to express conflict or agreement amongst themselves?
In fact were not stereotypes mainly used to define the terms of
an argument? Certainly, the marrowing of focus that stereotyping
implies can sharpen the contrasts that people may wish to employ
when making a point in argument: even community members could
be set at a distance, like strangers.

With regard to identity, what are people trying to prove
when they claim an identity? Do we not display different identities to different people so as to guide their reactions and thus
enable interaction to proceed? This is surely a case of manoeuver-
ing people for political needs in order to gain one's point. As
to defining and 'fixing' identity, is not the problem that identity
is a concept on the move that is infinitely adjustable to the present situation and hence has no stable meaning? As regards the
point that conscious deception may be employed in portraying a
given identity, were there not two other aspects to personal
identity - (i) the taken-for-granted aspect which is
purely habit; (ii) a pre-reflective   stage-
management/

management that governs our display of 'unconscious' signals
of identity? In other words, in our portrayal of identity
there are various levels of conscious attempts to make
evident who we are, not all necessarily deceptive or 'untrue'.
The fact that one found that people display   many identities
could be likened to the distinction between langue/parole
(language/speech) or even individual/community differences
and this display then calls for a similar treatment. Thus
there exists, for a given population, a repertoire of
identities but any individual is free to choose only certain
aspects of these identities in his everyday roles yet can
vary the composition to suit the particular needs of the
moment. Perhaps we should be more interested in the communally-
defined identities that are permitted rather than in any universal criteria. In the process of the individual construction of
identity one needs a reference group but, it should be noted,
this group is basically an ideological construct and not a
body of real people. Thus a knowledge of the permitted identities that a community allows would enable us to determine
what that ideological construct is.

Jackson's association of place with identity was also
queried for was not this only the case for rural communities?
With urban populations, by contrast, one typically has middle-
class inspired mobility where provenance sinks into insignifi-
cance. Another point was that rural identities (as expressed
by clothes or artefacts) were easily recognizable and it was
noticeable that urban people sometimes made use of such
'ethnic' items precisely in order to claim a (spurious)
link with the land, although with such usages, class
attitudes had also to be taken into account.

As/

As for naming, this process enables one to cope with other people's identity, for this knowledge gives power, but it is based on a system of classification just like occupational roles and hence could be learned by anyone; it is a reference grid for those who know the system. Regarding surnames, it was noteworthy that in bilingual areas the actual surname used was often quite arbitrary as it only fulfilled a bureaucratic necessity and was not employed locally anyhow. People were often named by reference to kinship - the son of A - where family stereotypes were often conjured up as explaining that person's behaviour. In those areas where bureaucratic necessity ruled there might only be a few surnames and hence kinship, locality or by-names (nicknames) were substituted by the locals. A further point to consider is the effect of a woman's legal change of name on marriage - what effect did this have on one's perception of her identity - was it kept separate or was it merged with her husband's? The suggestion was made that there was a great intersection of these various modes of naming and that no one single name was predominant - it was all relative to the situation. So the question was not so much about individual or group identity since the whole matter depended on the context in which it was employed.

As a semi-jocular proposal it was suggested that field-workers should try the experiment of denying that they had any name whatsoever and see what reaction they encountered? Curiously enough, the UK is one of the few societies that legally allows one to take any name one chooses, but it does insist that one is called something. Admittedly, one of the more endearing characteristics of the human species is that once you tell your name to people they endeavour to try to find/

find personal links with that name and hence to deny them
that privilege might be a bit hard.

2.   Varwell's paper to the seminar was different from that
published here but he still maintained that the themes of
way of life that he previously had identified; the personal,
corporate, cultural, historical - were closely related to
four other themes of relativity, identity, security and
exclusivity.

As it might be of interest to consider this elaboration
of Varwell's approach a summary of his theoretical points
and the subsequent discussion is included here.

In his seminar paper Varwell was concerned with testing
Cohen's model on identity (cf A. Cohen: "Social identity and
the management of marginality") which showed that social identity was used in marginal areas like Newfoundland and Shetland
for coping with large-scale social changes. Basically Cohen's
model of strategic adaptation can be seen at either the micro-
or macro-level in which either assertive or assimilative modes
are adopted. This model reduces to a 4-fold table where micro-
and macro-levels are related to assertive and assimilative
strategies.

Level	Assertive	Assimilative
Micro-	la	IIa
Macro-	lb	IIb

Strategy la stresses local values, lb wider values; IIa
stresses the need for modernization and the drive for improve-
ment at the local level, IIb emphasises the urban culture and
industrial development. Cohen argues that cutting across
these/

these four categories is an element of stigmatized introversion
whereby certain aspects of identity are avoided or dismissed.
This stigmatization occurs in certain areas because of a
hierarchical arrangement of occuptions there. The question
is whether this model applies to areas where change is not so
rapid and does it only apply to closed communities?

Varwell examined this model with regard to Fochabers in
Morayshire and concluded that Cohen's model held in places other
than those undergoing rapid change. In other words, Cohen's
model seemed to be generally applicable but the question was
raised whether in fact four _different_ strategies were being
followed?

The Harris Tweed industry was instanced as another example
that could be analysed according to Cohen's model. It was
regarded as being traditional (i.e. la) but in fact it was
invented fairly recently. As for category lb, Harris Tweed
was actually made in Lewis! Regarding point IIa it was at
the upper end of the market and said to be vital for locals
which, in fact, means only Stornoway or Lewis. Finally as to
point IIb, Harris Tweed was directed towards an international
market, primarily USA and Japan. The problem with this
particular case is the so-called contrasting categories. The
HIDB wished to modernize the industry but this was opposed
by the locals who pointed to the problems of overproduction
and high transport costs. Despite dire warnings of what
would happen if they did not modernize, _viz_.complete collapse,
the weavers did not heed this advice and seem to have been
coping successfully. As regards the stigmatization postulated,
there does not appear to be any observable hierarchy evolving
and hence no discrimination despite the basic insecurity of
weaving as an occupation. Thus this instance does not entirely
square with Cohen's model.

It/

It was also suggested that the situation of the distilleries in the Inner Hebrides was closer to the Harris Tweed situation and that again Cohen's model did not apply there either.

It is, of course, possible that people may hold part or all of the four views or strategies suggested in the model and that this might depend upon one's position in the hierarchy. The drawback with Cohen's model was its holistic nature, apparent to the observer, but not seen by any of the participants as a viable set of alternative strategies. This judgment is perhaps typical, whereby the informed outsider comes to conclusions that nobody in a specific situation can see. However, this is the strength of the outsider for he can often see more of the game than the players.

3.   Ennew's paper on self-image was deliberately not specific because identity was more a matter of ideas than of facts and hence it lacks precision since it cannot be unambiguously defined. The four principal constructs of Hebridean identity - the State, Academia, Tourism and the Hebrideans themselves - are all constructed around concepts of difference. Judgments on identity swing between good and bad images - the former being put out by Academia and Tourism while the darker side of life is recognized by the State (Welfare agencies) and the inhabitants. There is a basic insecurity in Hebridean identity that makes them hyper-sensitive to external criticism which partly arises from the constructs imposed upon them and the lack of fit with reality which these constructs have.

An interesting aspect was the impact of returnees, for they were often the most vocal in protesting against changes to the way of life and also objecting to the presence of outsiders. This situation was paralleled in Shetland where the returnees were more Shetland than Shetlanders, possibly because/

because they had made a break from traditional ties for
a while and could therefore be disloyal to the group and
be in favour of certain changes. This, of course, is
contradictory since one cannot support both the old way
of life and modern changes. Thus, some returnees place
themselves in a dilemma and please nobody. It is the break
with the community ties that gives such people self-
confidence and a determination to speak their minds but,
as we have seen, this does not always win acceptance. In
the Hebridean case, it is not simply economic reasons that
motivate returnees but a political zeal for Gaelic and the
fact that a new local authority has been set up which allows
islanders a certain degree of autonomy.

There are numerous conflicts of identity in the Hebrides -
the image of self-sufficiency yet a dependence on alcohol,
the occurrence of wife-beating yet the control of the purse-
strings by women. These conflicting images are, of course,
present in other areas of Scotland and not peculiar to the
Western Isles.

It was noted that in Shetland conversations often contained
references to conflict between incomers and locals in those
areas where there was a large influx of strangers. If constructs
of identity are ideological then there is likely to be a clash
when different sets of ideas are used to define identity in a
single place. Newcomers often try to redefine their identity
in the light of the situation they find themselves in but this
can easily lead to confusion. In Shetland, incomers tend to
be more critical of each other than of locals whereas in Lewis
incomers mainly complain about the locals. People tend to
attribute an unchangingness to identity and it was noticeable
that there was a greater stress on identity when that continuity
is/

is threatened by perceived threats of change. This may
explain some of the conflicts mentioned above.

4.   A paper relevant to this discussion is Cohen's "The
same - but different: The Allocation of Identity in Whalsay,
Shetland" in which he suggests it is the community that
allocates identity to its members rather than it being the
case that individuals create their own identity. If,
however, Cohen's point is correct then its effect is to
restrain the individual for the good of the community. The
question is whether this sociological view of harmony reflects
reality or whether it is only a theoretical construct!
Perhaps this allocation of identity only gives an illusion
of harmony. Is this allocation really an explanation anyway
or is it merely an empirical observation? It was agreed
that such a model of the allocation of identity may be true
for islands like Whalsay and Scalpay which have both a
natural and occupational (fishing) boundary. Certainly it
was the case that fishing communities had a need for co-
operation that aided the process of identity construction,
whether or not they were on an island. Fishermen seem to
form a special case for historical, legal and financial
reasons but their status and importance has changed consider-
ably this century. The effect of financial aid (from HIDB,
WFA, HIB, etc.,) has altered some of the traditional bonds
while the price of fish has greatly changed the income differ-
ential between fishermen and landsmen. When it comes to purely crofting communities nowadays these are kept going by an
ageing population only with the support of various subsidies,
allowances and pensions. As there are no economic pressures
to produce a higher yield, does this then affect the harmony
of crofting communities?

It/

It was objected that the idea of a harmonious community is an ideological construct, just as the egalitarian ethic itself is. Do people hold a collective image of contentedness and is this made by referring to the outside world? In the case of the Whalsaymen do they make their judgments in terms of the outside world all the time or only occasionally? The difficulty is that we are given no information of what the distinctive attributes of Whalsaymen are, so it is not possible to resolve these questions here. The problem with many ethnographic analyses is that their focus is so local; besides which, few comparisons are ever attempted even when the material exists. A case in point with the Whalsay study is that the analysis is totally male-oriented. Despite the fact that many wives come from the outside we do not learn how a woman acquires a Whalsay identity, if at all. This raises the general problem of sex-linked identities and the role of socialization.

In the case of Lewis it was noted that for incomers their boys did not integrate with local boys but girls were integrated with other girls while, paradoxically, all the men were integrated while the women were not. These differences arise partly because boys were competitive and the girls were not, while men cooperated but women were individualistic. These differences were not necessarily from choice since life-styles have changed more for women than for men. Today there are few communal tasks for women (like work on the croft, baking, washing, etc.) and so they tend to remain isolated in their tidy homes. This change must have posed problems of identity for women since they were clearly different from their grandmothers. Stemming from this uncertainty is the problem: what effect does all this have upon the children, since it is women who socialize children?

5./

5.   Turner's paper on Gala Day in a fishing village reveals a rigid ritualistic quality to the proceedings that has as its sole aim the maintenance of community stability. The interesting point is that the whole performance is staged by the children, even if it is supervised by Gala Day committee.

By contrast, many other Gala Days (e.g. in Fochabers) aim to raise money principally. Although these other occasions proclaim a local identity they are not devoid of social criticism for local figures are made fun of during the course of the proceedings. In fact, Cockenzie Gala Day, being a fairly recent innovation seems much too serious and self-conscious, possibly because it has no other function than a parade of virtue for the benefit of the children. It was questioned whether Turner's analysis was correct for there could be quite different interpretations of these events. If Gala Day is an expression of community identity it is not made clear of what exactly this identity consists nor how the ceremony supports that identity. An alternative version was promised and this is looked forward to with some interest.

6.   It will be noted that in the discussion a number of the questions remained unanswered. This is a good sign since it means that the papers have provoked a response and given everyone something further to investigate, which was the prime object of discussing these working papers. It is hoped that this publication will also cause readers to question their own ideas of way of life and identity. Bearing in mind the context of oil-developments in Scotland that has sharpened people's awareness of their way of life, this particular collection of papers lays the basis for further discussions of the impact of oil on small communities which will be explored in later issues in this series.

REFERENCES:

A Cohen   "Social identity and the management of Marginality"
in P G Sadler and G A Mackay (eds) The Changing
Future of Marginal Regions, Institute for the Study
of Sparsely Populated Areas, University of Aberdeen,
1977.

A Cohen   "'The same - but different': The allocation of
identity in Whalsay, Shetland". Sociological
Review 26:3, 1978.

NOTE:

The participants at the Second Way of Life Seminar (held in
Edinburgh University on May 19/20, 1979) were:

Judith Ennew (Cambridge)	Anthony Jackson (Edinburgh)
Graham McFarlane (Belfast)	Robert Turner (Edinburgh)
Adrian Varwell (Edinburgh)	James Wilson (Edinburgh).

This paper is one of a series published by the North Sea Oil Panel of the SSRC available from the address below using this page as an order form. Prices given are inclusive of post and packing, and your remittance should accompany the order.

Amount required

Paper No. 1 - "Social Change in Dunrossness: a Shetland Study" by R Byron and G Macfarlane, 152 pp, £1:80.

Paper No. 2 - "Oil and the Scottish Voter 1974-79" by W Miller, J Brand and M Jordan, 111 pp, £2:80.

Paper No. 3 - "North Sea Oil and the Aberdeen Economy" by G A Mackay and A C Moir, 105 pp, £2:80.

Paper No. 4 - "Way of Life and Identity" edited by A Jackson, 89 pp, £1:80.

Paper No. 5 - "Way of Life: in Search of Meaning" by A Varwell, 132 pp, £2:80.

Paper No. 6 - "The Highlands in Transition: Current Aspects of Social Geography in a Peripheral Area" by M B Cottam, P L Knox, and P H Hirsch, 116 pp, £2:80.

Paper No. 7 - "Labour Migration and Oil" edited by R Moore, 150 pp approx., £2:80.

To: North Sea Oil Panel, 2 The Square, University of Glasgow, Glasgow G12, Scotland.

I enclose a cheque for £ :   made payable to the North Sea Oil Panel.

Name . . . .

Address . . . .

       . . . .

       . . . .